The Dawn of Great Civilizations

Heralding the Return of the Mother Principle

By
Dr. Hilarion M. Henares, Jr.
Philippines

The Dawn of Great Civilizations
by Dr. Hilarion M. Henares Jr.

The Commonalities of Great Religions

Christianity
God the Father, The Son,
The Holy Spirit

Ancient Egypt
Isis, Mother Creator; Osiris, the
Consort, Horus, the Son

Hinduism
Vishnu the Creator; Shiva the
Destroyer,
Kali the Mother Principle

The Ten Commandments of Moses
The Basic Precepts of Isis
in the Egyptian Book of the Dead

Immaculate Conception
The unfertilized birth of Christ
Ancient Egypt
The birth of Horus from the missing
penis of Osiris

Christmas
The birth of the Son of God
Winter Solstice
The re-birth of the Sun

Easter
The Death and Resurrection of Christ
End of Winter and the Dying Year
The beginning of Spring and the
planting of new crops

Era of Darkness and Coming of the Light

Meet the prophet of the Era of Darkness and the Coming of the Light. In a sense he proclaims the idea of Death and Renewal, Crucifixion and Resurrection, End and Beginning that the New Year following our EDSA revolution, symbolizes to the Filipino of today. In his mind the ascendancy of President Cory Aquino represents in our country the re-affirmation of the Mother Principle, a sign that we may be emerging from darkness into the light.

His name is Michael Adams, and his very name evokes the passage of eons past since the beginning of time --- when Michael the Archangel battled the forces of darkness, when Jehovah took molecules of dust on the seventh day of Creation and shook them till their name was Adam. Michael Adams is an iconoclast, which means he is a destroyer of graven images, the annihilator of cherished traditions --- much like most great men of the human race, like Jesus who broke with Judaism, like Gandhi who broke with the gods of wrath, like Martin Luther King and Rolando Olalia. So Michael expects to suffer their fate. He will die, not of old age, but of a bullet in the brain. Michael Adams is an Englishman, a self-proclaimed genius who got his master's degree in history and law from Cambridge University at the age of 20, is married to a Filipina, made the Philippines his home, invested a fortune in Wise & Co. and Benguet Exploration, writes poetry, supports a community of artists, is 38 years of age and looks 70, with the added qualification that he is a dead ringer for Sidney Greenstreet dying of cirrhosis of the liver.

To Michael Adams, the Holy Trinity (God the Father, the Son and the Holy Spirit) is something common to most great religions. In Egypt there was the trinity of Isis the mother-creator, Osiris the consort, and Horus the son. In India, there is the trinity of Vishnu the creator, Shiva the destroyer and Kali the female principle. To Michael, the Ten Commandments of Moses is practically a direct copy of the Basic Precepts of Isis as enunciated in the Egyptian Book of the Dead. To Michael, the Immaculate Conception, the unfertilized birth of Jesus, had its parallel in the birth of Horus, whose father Osiris died with a missing penis, eventually discovered in the Nile. Isis then reconstructed the badly damaged Osiris, and had the child Horus with him even if he was a corpse. To Michael, even Christmas and Easter were adaptations of ancient traditions. Many scholars studying the position of the moon and stars, specially that of the planet Venus during the ancient times, concluded that Jesus must have been born sometime in October in the year 6 BC with Venus the "Evening Star" in its brightest ascendency as the Star of Bethlehem.

Why then was Christ's birthday designated December 25th? Because in the ancient calendar December 25th was the day of the Winter Solstice (in the new calendar, December 21st) which is the day when the sun is said to be born again. On that day, daylight is shortest, the night is longest; the days begin to lengthen, and the sun is said to be born again. In ancient religions, the male component of God is represented by the sun (Osiris), while the female is represented by the moon (Isis). In the eyes of the ancients, Christ the Messiah can only be born upon the rebirth of the sun. And why was Christ's death designated on Easter, a day with no definite date in the calendar occurring sometime in March or April? Because Easter corresponds to the ancient Festival of the End of the Dying Year, a tradition that started at the Temple of Nemi where ancients had the habit of sacrificing ruler-priests at that certain time of the year. "The King is dead. Long live the King!" is a tradition that stipulates that "Whoever kills The Priest becomes The Priest" and the death of the Old King symbolically fertilizes newly planted crops. Thus

"In the beginning was Isis, oldest of the old; she was the goddess from whom all becoming arose."

Thus was born the Cult of the Mother-Creator, the Mother Principle.

- Motherland
- Mother Nature
- Mother Earth
- Queen Bee
- Queen Ant

Under the Mother-Creator, Civilization flourished under
- The Greatness that was Egypt, for 3,000 years
- The Glory that was Greece, for 300 years
- The Grandeur that was Rome, for 1,229 years
- The Wonder that is China, for 4,012 years

Easter signaled the end of winter in Europe and the planting of new crops sometime in March and April, the day designated for the crucifixion and death of Christ the King.

"There in the beginning was Isis, oldest of the old; she was the goddess from whom all becoming arose." Thus started the Cult of Isis ten thousand years before Christ was born. According to Michael Adams, all religions were originally founded on the Female Principle, based on the concept of Mother-Creator --- a concept that still crops up when we speak of Mother Earth, Motherland, Mother Nature, and when we utter our first word "Mama!" In the insect world, we see the Queen Bee and Queen Ant from whom all existence emanates. For ten thousand years the Cult of Isis and its derivative forms were the dominant religion of the world, bringing civilizations to birth and flowering. Isis came in many forms: Myrionymos, Aruru, Artemis, Minerva, Hecate, Diktynna, Diana, Demeter Thesmophoros, Ariadne, Cybele, Hera, Nemesis, Ninhursag, Venus, Kali, our very own Haliya. Thus Lucius prayed to the Moon Goddess: *"Thou which dost illumine all the cities of the earth by thy feminine light!"* And in the Hindu Mantra: *"O Goddess Kali, he who makes an offering to you of pubic hair from his female partner pulled from the root, wet with semen poured from his penis into her menstruating vagina, becomes a great poet, a Lord of the world, and always travels on elephant-back."*

The Mother-Creator Goddess was a tolerant God, devoid of self-righteous bigotry and obsessive aversion to sex, democratic in her acceptance of all other gods into her pantheon. Under her benign guidance, agriculture and civilization was born in Egypt and the Near East; democracy, the arts, and the dignity of man came forth from the Glory that was Greece; modern government, public works, Justice and Equality before the law came forth from the Grandeur that was Rome. And today in the heartland of Asia, the spirit of *Ahimsa* and *Agape* still survives in our de-humanized world. *Ahimsa*: a reverence for life and reluctance to cause pain to any living creature. *Agape*: love for all men regardless of differences in race, color, or creed; the brotherhood of man based on our common humanity under the parenthood of God.

According to Michael Adams, Judaism and its two derivatives, Christianity and Islam, are Male-based and as such are perversions of the original Mother Principle, were intolerant of other religions, and were spread by subversion and the sword. God the Father-figure was the all-powerful King, the Great Dictator of heaven and earth, and "one cannot sue the priest for malpractice." The only saving grace of Christianity is the emergence of the Cult of Mary, the Mother of God, and that of Islam the Cult of Fatima, the daughter of Mohammed. The Jews are still ruled by a jealous and an avenging God, who designates quite unfairly and with uncharacteristic favoritism, the Jews as His Chosen People, distinct and separate from the rest of the world.

After lasting for more than 10,000 years, the Cult of Isis and its derivatives, its magnificent temples to the humanity of man, were destroyed when Rome was converted to Christianity. Christians were intolerant of their ancient heritage, and went berserk in an orgy of vandalism that had no parallel in all history. The collapse of Rome and its destruction came soon after Christianity became the world religion. The elimination of the Mother Principle was profoundly unsettling on human civilization, leading straight to the Dark Ages of the first millennium. Throughout those centuries of horror, a few monasteries and a magnificent library in Alexandria, Egypt, were the only keepers of the flame, the last refuge of civilization. The rest was a howling wilderness.

Golda Meir

Benazir Bhutto

Indira Gandhi

Aung San
Suu Kyi

Under Mother-directed Family-oriented religions of the Ancient World, different gods were tolerated in a common pantheon; absolutely no religious persecution.

DISPLACED BY
Father-directed, Alpha male oriented religions of Modern World, the same God under different names in different places of worship, Racial Discrimination, Religious Persecution, Institutionalized Genocide.

Signs of the Return of the Mother Principle:
- Political Tolerance, Goodwill and Compassion
- Emergence of Women Leaders
- Rise of Nuns within the Catholic Church
- The Surprising Strength and Endurance of the Cult of the Virgin Mary
- The Continuing Dominance of the most humane and most tolerant segment of the Church, the Society of Jesus.

Sirimavo
Bandaranaike

Angela Merkel

Margaret
Thatcher

Corazon
Aquino

It is ironical that for centuries, Catholics were forbidden to read the Bible, and forced to accept the Church as sole arbiter of faith and morals. Ironical too that at the time of the Renaissance, when civilization began to flower again, even church leaders looked for guidance and inspiration far back into the non-Christian world of Aristotle, Plato and Socrates; and adopted our numerals and basic sciences from the Arab world. "For some reason, Man must plant his fruit trees in the graveyard," wrote Catholic writer G.K. Chesterton.

According to Michael, a new Era of Darkness has descended upon the world with the death of Pope John XXIII and Pope John Paul I and the emergence of ultra Conservative and intolerant elements in the Church. In the book "In God's Name", it was alleged that John Paul I was poisoned because he was about to give away the wealth of the Church and change church policy on birth control. Michael believes that the way is being paved for the emergence of the Anti-Christ with his Opus Diaboli (excuse me, Opus Dei), accumulating wealth for a small elite and propping up fascist military regimes like those in Spain, Chile and recently in the Philippines.

According to Michael Adams, there are encouraging signs that the Mother Principle is coming back into the world. First, the emergence of great women leaders, such as Siri Bandaranaike, Golda Meir, Indira Gandhi, Margaret Thatcher, and in the Philippines, Corazon Aquino. Second, the surprising strength of the Cult of Mary, which has so far weathered massive assaults from the Fundamentalist, Pentecostal and Television evangelists such as Brother Ray Orosa, Pat Robertson and Jerry Falwell. Third, the assertion of the Mother Principle within the church itself, in the Philippines personified by the wonderful Sisters Christine Tan, Aurora Zambrano, Mary John Mananzan, Mariani Dimaranan. Fourth, the continuing dominance of the most tolerant and humane segment of the Church, the Society of Jesus. "I would not be a Catholic if not for the Jesuits," said Michael Adams, adding, "Everyone should have a Jesuit of his own."

True. Michael has Father John Steinbugler. I have Father James Reuter, my mother and sister have Father Jaime Bulatao; President Cory Aquino has Father Catalino Arevalo; Jimmy Ongpin has Father Joaquin Bernas, Imelda Marcos and Vince Valdepeñas had Father Michael McPhelin; Emmanuel Soriano had Father John P. Delaney, Johnny Tan and Jerry Montemayor had Father Walter B. Hogan; a couple of women took possession of Father Samuel Wiley and Father Leo Larkin; and Hilario Lim had Father Fritz Araneta. The only unsettling thing is the fact that Minister Juan Ponce Enrile has exchanged Jesuit Father James Reuter for a new spiritual adviser, former Don Bosco Father Antony Pezzota, who recently abandoned his priesthood to become a married man and Baptist Minister. In his testimony, Reverend Pezzota rejected Mary as the Mother of God.

But Michael Adams, the prophet of our times, ever cognizant of the fact that false prophets are stoned and thrown off the cliff, confidently predicts that in spite of Opus Diaboli and the Fundamentalist sects, the Mother Principle will in good time gain ascendancy and herald in our time and place, the Coming of the Light.

President Ferdinand Edralin Marcos from his perch as dictator of the Philippines, during 14 years of Martial Law. Today on August 15, 2016, I found 100 persons on Facebook named Michael Adams, none of which is the one mentioned above, who if alive, should be 66 years old today.

Timeline

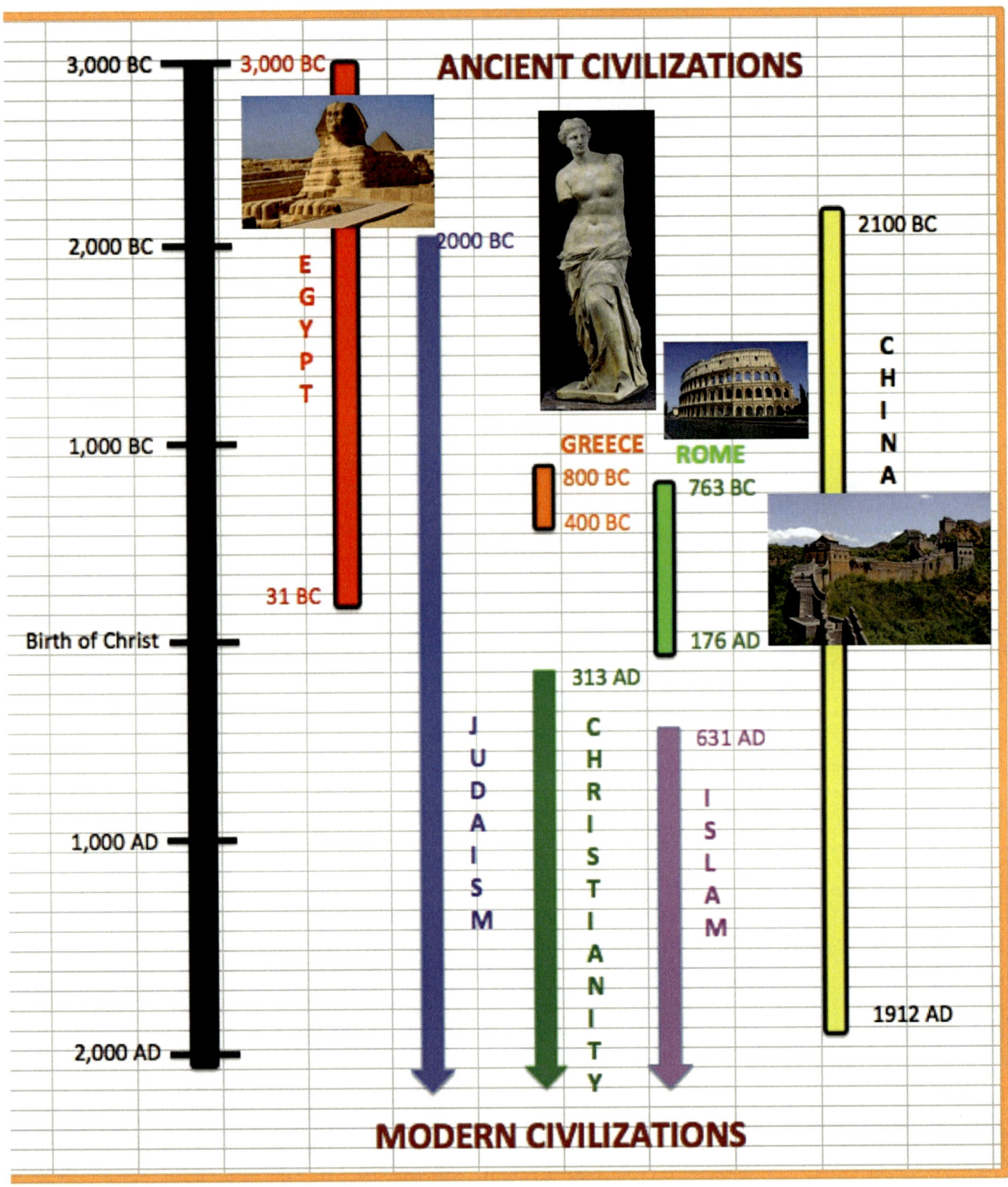

ANCIENT CIVILIZATIONS

3,000 BC

3,000 BC

EGYPT

2,000 BC

2000 BC

2100 BC

CHINA

1,000 BC

GREECE

ROME

800 BC

763 BC

400 BC

31 BC

176 AD

Birth of Christ

313 AD

631 AD

JUDAISM

CHRISTIANITY

ISLAM

1,000 AD

1912 AD

2,000 AD

MODERN CIVILIZATIONS

The Dawn of Great Civilizations

The Egyptian Civilization existed for almost 3,000 years, from 3,000 BC to 31 BC when Cleopatra died; the Greatness that was Ancient Egypt saw the birth of Agriculture, the making of a written language, and the legitimacy of rulers, of Pharoahs who ruled dynasty after dynasty, and produced engineering marvels of such magnitude and magnificence as the Pyramids.

The Greek Civilization existed for only 300 years between 800 BC to 500 BC when the city-state was born; but the Glory that was Ancient Greece contributed more than any ancient civilization that ever existed, to philosophy (Aristotle, Socrates, Plato, Anaxagoras), to sculpture (Phidias, Praxiteles), to governance and statesmanship (Pericles, Themistocles), to theater (Dionysius, Aeschylus, Euripides, Aristophanes), to science ((Archimedes, Pythagoras, Anaximander), to history (Herodotus), to medicine (Hippocrates), and to poetry (Homer), that a historian was moved to remark, "It is as though the individuality of Greek Civilization strove for a brief period of its maturity, to **surpass the bounds of possible achievement**."

The Roman Civilization existed for 1,229 years from Romulus the first king of Rome (753 BC) to the German prince Odoacer, the first King of Italy (176 AD); the Grandeur that was Ancient Rome endured with the codification of Roman Law and Roman Justice available to every Roman Citizen, *Fiat Justicia, ruat coelum!* – Let Justice be done though the heavens fall! Its military might and engineering genius that invented the arch, the vault and the dome, and built bridges, aqueducts and paved roads to the far reaches of the empire, ensured its longevity.

The Chinese Civilization existed for 4,012 years from the Xia Dynasty (2100 BC) to Sun Yat-Sen's Republic (1912 AD), co-existing with ALL the ancient civilizations of Egypt, Greece and Rome and outlasting them all; The Wonder that was Ancient China endured because it was insulated from all threats of invasion by the Gobi Desert on the West, the Great Wall on the North, the Pacific Ocean on the East and the Himalayas on the South – and ruled a homogenous population united by the teachings of two Great Teachers, Confucius and Buddha (imported from India where it started in 620 BC). In comparative isolation, China was able to build a civilization that pioneered in the creation of a Civil Service bureaucracy, and invented most of the technological advances that the West countries re-invented and claimed as its own.

What is the common trait that characterizes the Egyptian, Greek, Roman and Chinese Civilizations? It is their religions, a multiplicity of gods that co-exist in common pantheons, Family-oriented and Mother-directed religions that welcome all gods and their worshippers without bigotry or discrimination.

There are as much as 2,000 gods in Ancient Egypt, many of them come in families – Osiris and Isis and son Horus; Shu and Tefnut, with twins Geb and Nut; and Creators Atum, Re, Ptah and Khnum and Khepri.

The Ancient Greeks and Ancient Romans shared a pantheon of 12 gods on Mount Olympus headed by father Zeus (or the Roman equivalent, Jupiter) and mother Hera (or Juno) and an entire family of Gods: Poseidon (or Neptune), Cronus (or Saturn), Aphrodite (or Venus), Hades (or Pluto), Hephaistos (or Vulcan), and others.

ANCIENT RELIGIONS
Different and multiple gods in a common pantheon, religious tolerance

Egypt
2,000 gods led by Isis, Osiris & Horus

Greece and Rome

12 gods on Mount Olympus giants and semi-gods led by Zeus (Jupiter)

China
200 gods and goddesses led by the Dragon King, Confucius as Teacher

MODERN RELIGIONS
Same God in different places of worship, religious intolerance, racial discrimination, institutionalized genocide. Holy wars

- **Judaism**
  Yahweh, or Jehovah

- **Christianity**
  The Holy Trinity with God the Father, the Son and the Holy Spirit

- **Islam**
  Allah

And there were Titans, Giants, and others. The Olympics was a religious exercise introduced by the Greeks in 776 BC and continued by the Romans. 293 Olympiads were held, once every four years, for 1,170 years; and ended in 394 AD when it was abolished during the reign of Roman Emperor Theodosius the Great.

There are over 200 gods and goddesses in Ancient China who created the world and human beings, and kept them functioning, each with its own power and influence, oldest of whom is the Dragon King, a wise old man who also takes the shape of a dragon. One of its religions is Buddhism introduced in 67 AD from India, praying to a multitude of gods such as Guanyin and Deva, bringing the concepts of reincarnation, retribution and compassion towards all living things. But the most powerful influence on the Chinese even up to the present is that of Kongzi or Confucius, a teacher and philosopher who was born in September, 551 BC, and who championed strong family loyalty, ancestor worship, respect of elders by their children and of husbands by their wives. He also recommended the family as a basis for ideal government. He espoused the well-known principle "Do not do to others what you do not want done to yourself," the Golden Rule.

These Family oriented, Mother-directed religions were common to all these ancient civilizations. There is a whale of difference between these Mother-directed religions, and the Father-directed religions that followed in their wake – Judaism and its derivatives, Christianity and Islam. Mothers are more inclined to unconditional love, are less judgmental, being the nurturer of the human race have less aversion to sex, and are more willing to accept all gods without bigotry or discrimination. Fathers, especially the Alpha-male, are more judgmental, more inclined to justice and retribution than human compassion, more supportive of a jealous and avenging God who encourages tribal loyalties, favoritism toward his Chosen People, and who insists, "I am the Lord thy God, thou shall not have any strange gods before me."

It is ironic to observe that the people of these ancient civilizations have DIFFERENT strange gods to worship, but never engaged in religious persecution, while people of modern religions – of Jewish, Christian and Muslim faiths -- worshipping the SAME God – Yahweh, God the Father, and Allah – have been at each other's throats for 20 centuries, splitting into different sects that torture and torch each other throughout modern history – Christians into Catholic and thousands of Protestant sects, Muslim into Sunnis and Shiites. Jews in the modern era are divided into Reform, Conservative and Orthodox sects of Judaism, but they are too few and have far too many outside enemies to engage in internecine warfare. Modern peoples worship the same God, and cannot stand each other. Ancient peoples worship different gods, and tolerate each other.

The coming of the Father-directed religions – Judaism, Christianity and Islam -- had a profound effect on the human race. For it ushered into play new and extremely disturbing concepts: unrelenting rivalry, competition and persecution among religions; something that never existed before, notions of racial superiority and genocide; and ideological warfare between different schools of thought, Capitalism versus Socialism, Democracy versus Dictatorship, Rights of Man versus Divine Right of Kings.

Ancient wars were fought by professional armies, according to established rules of combat, and non-combatants were merely part of the spoils of war, who hardly cared who eventually ruled them. Modern wars are fought by entire populations, non-combatants became refugees begging to be saved. And with the rise of technologies, wars became truly World Wars, and Holy Wars.

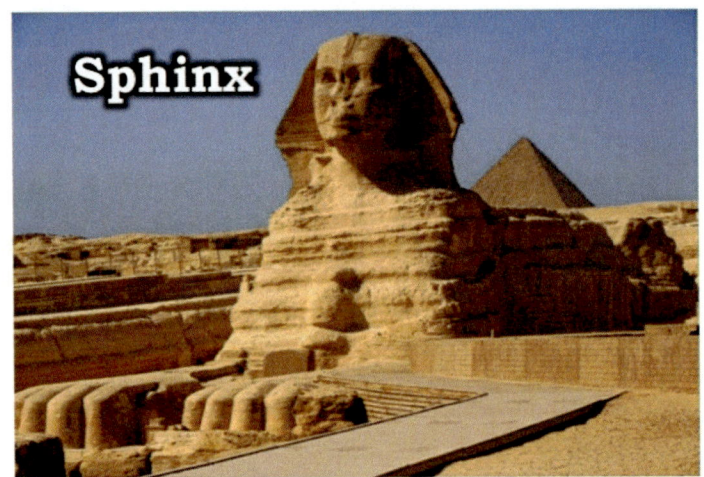

Sphinx

Rosetta Stone

The Pyramids

Nefertiti

Tutankhamen

The Greatness that was Egypt

My wife, daughter and I were there where history began, in Egypt, on the plateau of Gizah where three pyramids stand as the mightiest of all human achievements. No traveler -- emperor, merchant or poet -- has looked on them and the Sphinx and not gasp with awe. When dawn comes, as it did for centuries, the Sphinx will watch the Sun-god rise on the far bank of the Nile, its face turned towards its rays, and if we all listen, we shall hear it speak to us across the centuries, as in *Son et Lumiere:*

For five thousand years, I, the Sphinx, have seen all the suns men can remember come up in the sky. I saw the history of Egypt in its first glow, as tomorrow I shall see the East burning with a new flame. Through the ages I received many names: Harmachis, Horus, Lord of the Desert, Lord of the Heavens, Sovereign of Eternity. But the name which has remained with me is that given to me by a Greek traveler, the Father of History, the historian Herodotus. He called me Sphinx, and that name is now mine.

Here I stand at the foot of mountains of stone before which man looks like an insect. Yet it was men who built these massive monuments, and the names of the Pharoahs, whose tombs they are, have come down the ages. There is the greatest of all pyramids, that of Cheops of the Fourth Dynasty, 4,000 years ago. The area it covers is vast enough to hold St. Peter's Cathedral in Rome, and those of Florence, Milan, Westminster Abbey and St. Paul's. There are the pyramids of Chephren and Menkaure, smaller but more impressive in design.

Through the millenniums, dynasty succeeded dynasty. But among all the monarchs of ancient Egypt, none is more appealing than a young Pharoah, poet and mystic, who called himself Ikhnaton and who founded the first religion of The One God, long before the Jewish Jehovah ever impinged on the mind of Man. By his side was wife Nefertiti, whose image of beauty has come to us in stone. And his successor Tutankhamen, who died not yet twenty, and whose youthful face comes to us from the only tomb unravaged by robbers, in the Valley of the Kings.

I the Sphinx,who know the untouchable stars, have seen conquerors reflect before me and bow their heads. I saw Alexander the Great, handsome barbarian, thoughtful as a prophet. I saw Julius Caesar one evening for he feared the sun. Our last queen Cleopatra bore him a child. I saw Napoleon and his burning eyes. Centuries passed over my forehead. Yet these great men raised no more than dust.

I have known years of despair. An emir of the Middle Ages disliked my smile, and had me disfigured by his artillery. Then children found me ugly. No longer did anyone listen to me.

The keys of Old Egypt were lost. I was nearly buried in sand. All our knowledge, our very soul rolled in thousands of papyri, was sleeping unknown and unintelligible in dark and silent tombs. Yet the miracle did happen, in 1799, near Rosetta, where one of Napoleon's officers discovered a stone, a monolith bearing an edict issued by Ptolemy, the ancestor of Cleopatra. The inscription was in Greek and in hieroglyphs -- which enabled a Frenchman Champollion to decipher the lost tongue of Ancient Egypt.

Statues of Ramses II

Life in Ancient Egypt

Battle of Actium

Suicide of Cleopatra

Anthony & Cleopatra

Then it was like a resurrection! All at once, hieroglyphs were born to new life. Herons, lotus flowers, fishes, hares and drakes, the mysterious characters suddenly woke up, fluttered and sung like creatures of the fields as the sun rises. Unearthed from their deep silence, the papyri rustled with a hundred voices. From their leaves even rises the voice of the first schoolboys who struggled to write: *Master, because you beat me I have learnt my lesson... Child, offer your thanks to God.* And learned men were enthralled when in maxims and proverbs, they found wisdom as ancient as the pyramids, and as eternally young... *The plans of men never wholly succeed, but only what God has ordained. Beware of women, the room where they sit is full of ill-feelings. Do not answer good by evil. Justice comes before strength.* And historians were moved because so many centuries later they were reading, yes, love letters. *I can no longer touch your heart, why? -- You are there with me everywhere. With every step. -- My whole life hangs on your lips. Seeing you is better than eating or drinking.* Such is my message from the depths of the ages. And if these voices seem familiar, it is because their first echo had already reached you through Greece, Rome, Christianity and Islam.

The picture that emerges from the hieroglyphs is of a culture with few equals in the beauty of its art, the accomplishment of its architecture or the richness of its religious traditions. We were the first to learn how to plant and domesticate animals, taming the flood waters of the Nile for irrigation. We were the the first to institutionalize great reverence for the dead and belief in life after death, the first to develop the all-important ideology of kingship (the divine right of kings), and the first to develop the art of writing. Imhotep, an architect, priest and healer, built the world's first major stone building, the Step-Pyramid at Saqqara. Pyramid-building proliferated and reached its zenith with the construction of the Great Pyramid of Cheops at Giza.

We were ruled by women too: Queen Sobekneferu (1789-1786 B.C.), the first confirmed female ruler of Egypt; Queen Hatshepsut (1503-1482 B.C.), regent for her stepson Thutmose III, Egypt's greatest military hero, but rose to wield all the powers of a pharaoh; the legendary Cleopatra VII who surrendered Egypt to Rome in 31 BC, after which Egypt became a Roman province.

We were ruled by foreigners too, but like China, we absorbed them and civilized them. Around 1650 B.C., a line of foreign rulers known as the Hyksos took advantage of Egypt's instability to take control. The Hyksos rulers of the 15th dynasty adopted and continued many of the existing Egyptian traditions in government as well as culture. The 22nd dynasty began around 945 B.C. with King Shoshenq, a descendant of Libyans who had invaded Egypt during the late 20th dynasty and settled there. In the eighth century B.C., Nubian pharaohs beginning with Shabako, ruler of the Nubian kingdom of Kush, established their own dynasty–the 25th–at Thebes. Persian rulers such as Darius (522-485 B.C.) ruled the country largely under the same terms as native Egyptian kings: Darius supported Egypt's religious cults and undertook the building and restoration of its temples. In the mid-fourth century B.C., the Persians again attacked Egypt, reviving their empire under Artaxerxes III in 343 B.C. Barely a decade later, in 332 BC, Alexander the Great of Macedonia defeated the armies of the Persian Empire and conquered Egypt. After Alexander's death, Egypt was ruled by a line of Macedonian kings, beginning with Alexander's general Ptolemy and continuing with his descendants down to the last Pharoah, Cleopatra.

Tomorrow once more the sun will give me, the Sphinx, its first caress. Thousands of other suns shall rise again, and man's oldest achievements will remain. Yet in the course of time, even these pyramids will crumble. But the spirit which conceived them will never perish.

Oracle at Delphi

Venus de Milo

Hippocrates,
Father of Medicine

Archimedes
Eureka!

The Glory that was Greece

"The Greeks are children. Clever of course, but still children," said the Egyptian priest to a Greek named Solon, as recorded by Plato, in the year 600 before Christ. At the time the Egyptian Colossus still stood, as it did 3,000 years before, but it was already in the last stages of decay, its "splendor of life had boiled over and wasted into steam and froth." Looking east, the Egyptian would see the ruins of other empires – the Hittites, the dreaded Assyrians were gone; mighty Babylon and mighty Egypt about to be absorbed into the Persian Empire.

As for the Greeks, they were everywhere – in Egypt, Syria, Asia Minor, in hundreds of colonies scattered in the Aegean Islands and along the coasts from Marseilles to the Black Sea. They were an intelligent people, good mercenary soldiers, keen traders and skilled craftsmen. But there was also something irritating about their perpetual curiosity. They were brave warriors and expert sailors, but far from falling in line behind a king like the obedient Egyptians and Babylonians, they could rarely be persuaded to even to follow their own clan leaders for long; they were perpetually quarrelling among themselves. The trouble was that they would argue and regard themselves as "free men" – whatever that meant.

"The Greeks are children, clever of course, but still children," said the Egyptian priest, as he would return to his temple to perform once again the sacred rites which his predecessors had been practicing since the dawn of history. *He* did not ask questions. His ancestors had provided all the answers more than 3,000 years ago.

The most perplexing contradiction in the character of the Ancient Greeks is between their capacity for rational thought, and their adherence to what we regard as the grossest superstition. They were probably the most intelligent and knowledgeable people that ever lived. They were founders of what we call "science"; they observed, studied and reasoned out things. They discovered the true nature of eclipses, that the world was round, and that, like the other planets, the earth revolved around the sun. They conducted deep inquiries about the origin of matter, calling the primal substance *"physis"* (nature, hence our word "physics"), made up of indivisible particles (from *"atomos"*, meaning indivisible, comes our word "atom").

Yet these same brilliant people respected oracles, and could base vital decisions – such as whether or not to resist the Persians, and therefore whether or not Western Civilization should survive – on the babblings of an old woman squatting in a cave at Delphi, chewing laurel leaves. There was never a unified Greek state. Partly because of the geography of the country, divided as it was, by high mountains and sea channels running deep inland, and partly due to the character of the people themselves, the Greek ideal of government became the small, independent city state which they called *"polis"*; it is from this incidentally and related Greek words such as *"polites"* (citizen) and *"politeia"* (citizenship) that we derive our words "political" – pertaining to the state or its government – and "politician" – one allegedly skilled in politics. To the Greeks, the state was the city and its surrounding areas, most of them small.

Except for Sparta, the Greeks were not ruled by kings. They experimented with various forms of government, usually elective: sometimes an oligarchy (rule by a few), sometimes an aristocracy which originally meant "rule by the best" (from *"aristos"*, best and *"kratia"* rule), but often one man would seize power and became an absolute ruler (autocrat).

Socrates drinking hemlock poison

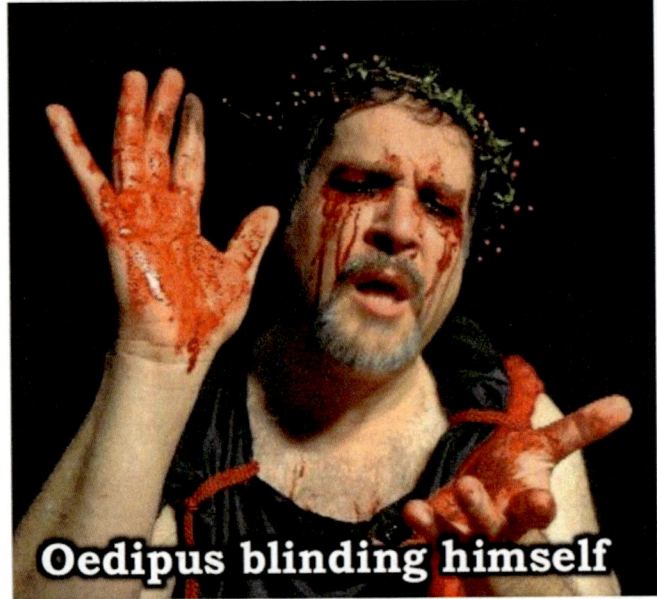

Oedipus blinding himself

Orestes pursued by the Furies

Pericles of Athens

The Greeks discovered –as who has not? – that such men are often corrupted by power, then the Greeks gave them the less complimentary name of "*turranikos*" (tyrant), meaning a cruel and oppressive ruler; and it became an act of patriotism to destroy them. The most popular form of government – in every sense of the word – was "*demokratia*" (rule by the people) which reached its greatest glory in Athens 450 years before Christ. From it comes our word "democracy". It is significant that all our words describing systems of government came from the Greek language.

The Greek ideal was the full complete man, daring, adventurous, sexy, successful in many fields of activity, in which wealth is acquired was merely incidental. The finest in the Greek spirit showed itself in other ways. It took the dross of barbaric myth and the earth of folktale, and transmuted it into the pure gold of poetry. In the hands of Aeschylus, Euripides and Sophocles, poetic myth became an instrument which searched men's hearts and souls, making them see the splendor and the meanness, the tragedy and comedy of human life. The Oresteian trilogy of Aeschylus tells the story of cannibalism, human sacrifice, murder, matricide – as barbarous and inhuman as any folktale from Egypt. Yet Aeschylus transforms it into one of the greatest tragedies of the world, exploring the heights which the human spirit can attain, and the miry depths to which it can sink; its message, the futility of revenge, of violence breeding violence, war breeding war, is as pertinent today as it was 2,500 years ago.

"We love things of the mind," the Athenians used to say, and sat at the feet of teachers and philosophers, Socrates, Plato and Aristotle. The ordinary Athenians, men and women, who crowded the open-air theater of Dionysus, on the slope of the Acropolis, did not mind being asked to think. Not that they went there for culture. They went there to be entertained. In the theater of Dionysus – the birthplace of Western drama – they sat happily munching their figs and pomegranates, and was played out before them the tragedies of Aeschylus, Euripides' satires on public men (where politicians are subjected to barbs and lampoons, as in our modern Press Gridiron affairs). And they roared at the comedies of Aristophanes – sex comedies of such outrageous, glorious wit.

The classical Greeks were a different kind of human beings from any other that preceded them -- the Egyptians, the Sumerians, the Assyrians, the Babylonians – different in the art, their literature, moral outlook, political organization, in their way of thinking, and feeling about life.

How did they get that way? First, they were great travelers and wherever they went they came in contact with earlier, older cultures which they approached with fresh curious minds untrammeled by traditions. Secondly, there was the so-called "genius of the race". Since men first achieved civilization there has never been such a flowering of genius as occurred, within one century, in Athens of 450 BC.

In a city no larger than San Francisco – only three generations produced such tragic poets as Aeschylus, Euripides and Sophocles, and the comic poet Aristophanes; philosophers such as Socrates, Plato, Aristotle, Anaxagoras; the great Herodotus, the father of historians; the sculptors Phidias and Praxiteles; and statesmen of the quality of Pericles and Themistocles. These were only the most distinguished. There are many others who, in a less brilliant age, would have shone as brightly as Christopher Marlowe and Ben Johnson might have done, had they not lived in the Age of William Shakespeare.

Messenger bringing news of Greek victory at Marathon

Greek victory at the Battle of Salamis

Parthenon – Original View

Parthenon Today

A historian once remarked: "It is as though the individuality of the Greek civilization strove for a brief period of its maturity to surpass the bounds of possible achievement."

The ancient Greeks were a race of individualists. But this was a strength and a weakness, for while the Greek love of freedom gave full play to the growth of the spirit and of the intellect encouraging the gifted and the intelligent, it hindered them from uniting and sinking their differences in the face of a common enemy, except on one rare and wonderful occasion.

The victory of the Greeks at Marathon and Salamis over the Persian brand of colonial Imperialism did not bring the millennium to Greece. Greek individualism and self-interest, the stubborn pride that had beaten the barbarian, broke up in the end the precious unity Athens had striven to create. Greek fought Greek, for power, for possession of land, out of jealousy of Athen's dominance. Men fought and died bravely, but year after year the Hellenic world dissipated its strength in war. And weakened, it was finally destroyed. But that is another story.

The ancient Greeks are a people whom we recognize, and who, despite many differences, think, act and speak like us. One not only admires, but loves them – and despairs for them. They had all our faults; perhaps we have a few of their virtues – one hopes so.

We who travel to Greece, as Herodotus once travelled to the ancient civilizations of Egypt and Babylon, may find in Greece the very roots of our being.

We find here the remains of temples and monuments, still standing, gloriously arrayed by the majesty of time. It seems that the flower of youth throbs within them, which time cannot quell, as if there flowed through their stone the immortal breath of a soul rebellious to age.

And as we gaze at the Acropolis high on the crest of a towering rock of ages, we hear the echo of words spoken down the corridors of time. And if we listen carefully, they seem to be saying to us especially:

I am the Glory that was Greece. For centuries past and for eons to come, I shall stand for order, law and clarity. I shall be a manner of thought, of love, of reason.

Lifting their eyes towards me, philosophers shall discover the depths of thought, architects shall dream of the majesty of their palaces.

So come to me, all you truth-seekers.

Come to this consecrated rock – where truth, virtue and infinite beauty have mingled to give birth to the Consciousness of Man.

Hannibal crossing the Alps

Assassination of Julius Caesar

Mark Anthony's
Funeral Oration for Julius Caesar

The Grandeur that was Rome

The Roman civilization existed for 1,200 years, shifting from a <u>Monarchy</u> to an oligarchic Republic to a immense Empire. It began as a city founded on seven hills by twins Romulus and Remus, who were raised by a she-wolf, who had a quarrel that ended with Romulus killing Remus and naming the city after himself. Thus established, Rome existed as a monarchy with seven kings from 763 to 509 BC when the king's son Sextus raped a virtuous woman named Lucrecia who then committed suicide. In response, four Romans headed by a man named Brutus, incited a rebellion and turned over the City of Rome as a Republic to the Senate and the people, and forever after, the term King had an unfavorable connotation for the Romans.

Rome as a Republic in a few hundred years expanded its control over most of the Italian Peninsula. It came into conflict with another power, a Greek nation called Carthage, located in what is now Tunisia. Unlike Rome which focused on a land-based military at the expense of their navy, Carthage had perhaps the most powerful fleet in the world. Things came to a head in a conflict over the island of Sicily, a colony of Carthage. In 264 BC the first of three Punic Wars began, and raged for 23 years, and ended in a draw because Rome could not cross over to the island for fear of Carthage's powerful fleet, and Carthage could not combat Rome's powerful army. But Rome was able to modernize its navy and take the fight to Africa. And in 241 BC, Carthage surrendered, and left Rome with the most powerful force in the Mediterranean. The new peace did not last however and in 218 BC the Second Punic War began. The German barbarian Hannibal crossed the Alps with his army of elephants into Italy and wreaked havoc in Rome. In 202 BC the Roman general Scipio defeated Hannibal, went to Africa once more and defeated Carthage, ending the Second Punic war in 201 BC, and expanding Roman influence over Spain and Greece. Carthage, now a Roman vassal, was invaded by the neighboring kingdom of Numidia. Since Carthage was forbidden to have its own troops after the Second Punic War, it asked Rome for help as she was supposed to. The Romans with a reputation for duplicity, invaded Carthage once more, attacked a militia Carthage raised for self defense, burned Carthage to ashes, scattered salt on the ground so that nothing can grow there, and Carthage was no more, after the Third Punic War.

By the mid-2nd century BC, Rome controlled the west Mediterranean, policing and defending it with massive armies. The troops had more loyalty to the generals than to distant politicians, giving men like Marius, Sulla, Pompey and Julius Caesar the muscle to seize political power. Meanwhile, peasants, whose land had been destroyed during the invasion of Hannibal in 219 BC, had flooded into Rome. They were followed by slaves and freedmen from conquered lands such as Greece, swelling the population to half a million. There was plenty of work for immigrants, constructing roads, aqueducts, markets and temples, financing by taxes on Rome's expanding trade. Rome owed much of her prosperity to her skilled civil engineers. When the city's wells were no longer sufficient, aqueducts were built to bring water from surrounding hills, some over 80 km long.

Julius Caesar, fresh from triumphs in the Gallic Wars (*Veni, Vedi, Vici,* he reported, I came, I saw, I conquered), adding modern France and Belgium to the Empire, "crossed the Rubicon" river, without disbanding his army, defying the authority of the Senate, and marched on Rome. He defeated the republican forces under Pompey who fled to Egypt where he was assassinated. Caesar with Mark Antony followed, and promptly started an affair with Cleopatra who bore him a son. Caesar was now master of Rome and made himself consul and dictator. He used his

Caligula and his horse

Pompeii

Nero and the burning of Rome

power to carry out much-needed reform, relieving debt, enlarging the senate, building the Forum Julium and revising the calendar. Dictatorship was always regarded a temporary position but in 44 BC, Caesar took it for life. His success and ambition alienated strongly republican senators, who led by Cassius and Brutus, assassinated Caesar on the Ides (15th) of March 44 BC. This sparked the final round of civil wars which ended in the defeat of Mark Antony and Cleopatra by Octavian in the Battle of Actium. This ended the Republic and brought about the elevation of Caesar's great nephew and designated heir, Octavian, as Augustus, the first emperor.

The reign of Augustus Caesar was the golden age of the Roman Empire, ushering the known world into *Pax Romana*, and to the birth of Christ. "Roman Empire" can also be known as *"Imperium Romanum"*, probably the best-known Latin expression where the word imperium simply means "territory"; the Roman Empire represents that part of the world under Roman rule. The expansion of this Roman territory beyond the borders of the initial city-state of Rome had started long before the state organization turned into an Empire. In its territorial peak after the conquest of Dacia by Trajan, the Roman Empire controlled approximately 5,900,000 km^2 (2,300,000 sq.mi.) of land surface, thereby being one of the largest empires during classical antiquity.

But what kept the Empire running are the throngs of slaves who worked everywhere: in Roman mines, fields, and households. Many came as war captives; others were born into bondage. And while the ancient institution of slavery festered with the same abuses seen later in American history, in the Roman Empire it had a different complexion. Slavery was not based on race. In fact, it was what you could call an equal opportunity condition. Anyone was liable to become a slave at any time. And, in fact, the biggest difference between ancient forms of slavery and modern forms of slavery is this absence of a sharp color contrast. There were no notions of racial superiority or institutional genocide as happened in America and Australia. Roman slaves merged so well into the population that the Senate once considered a plan to distinguish them by special dress. The idea was rejected. If slaves saw how numerous they were, the Senate decided, they might be emboldened to rebel. The Grandeur of Ancient Rome is not in its Coliseum and aqueducts, but in its roads, straight and true, leading to Rome from all directions, bringing civilization and centralized government to barbarians, bringing them Roman law and Roman justice that is the right of every Roman citizen.

There were several reasons for the decline of Roman Empire. They are all interweaved with each other. Decline in morals and values, public health problems, political corruption, unemployment, inflation, urban decay, inferior technology, military spending. All these facts had contributed to the fall of one of the greatest ancient civilizations. The decline of Rome is studded with many stories: of Caligula who appointed his horse a Consul; of Nero who murdered his own mother, played his fiddle while Rome burned, and fed Christians to the lions; and the saga of the city of Pompeii which in 79 AD was buried in the ashes of volcanic eruptions by Mount Vesuvius. In 1748, the site was rediscovered; underneath a thick layer of dust and debris, Pompeii was mostly intact. The buildings, artifacts and skeletons left behind in the buried city have taught us a great deal about everyday life in the ancient world. Pompeii was a flourishing resort for Rome's most distinguished citizens. Elegant houses filled with paintings and elaborate villas lined the paved streets. Tourists, townspeople and slaves bustled in and out of small factories and artisans' shops, taverns and cafes, and brothels (signs of male penises pointed the way) and bathhouses. People gathered in the 20,000-seat arena and lounged in the open-air squares and marketplaces.

Marco Polo in the Court of Kublai Khan

The Great Wall of China

Life-sized Terracotta Army

The Wonder that was China

China, the world's oldest surviving civilization, is still an enigma to the world. In Venice of the 13th century, people referred to Marco Polo as "Il Millone"-- the man who talked in millions, as he related fabulous tales of his 26 years at the golden courts of the great Kublai Khan. The journey took more than three years -- from the Crusader city of Acre in 1273 with his father and uncle through caravan trails that led to the salt mountains of Talkhan, to Kashmir, to Badakhshan with its mountains of rubies and emeralds; the great plains of Pamir, so high no birds could fly there; the splendid Samarkand with its Christian Church miraculously supported in thin air; the great Gobi desert, where spirit voices lured the unwary traveler to his doom. Yet none of these marvels could compare with Kinsai (now Hangchow), like Marco's native Venice, built upon lagoons of water and intersected by canals. Yet all of Venice, at the time the greatest city on Europe, would have fitted into one of Kinsai's 12 quarters. Kinsai was more than a hundred miles in circumference, with a main street 200 feet wide from one end of the city to the other, broken every four miles by large squares lined with palaces, gardens and shops. With high stone bridges under which full-masted vessels could pass, crowded with silk-clad lords and beautiful women, with shops full of spices, pearls and silks, with a great lake studded with wooded islands and pleasure pavilions, Kinsai boasted of a royal palace many times larger and richer than any in which a European king slept. To the nearby seaport of Zaiten (Chuan-chiao), thousands of Chinese junks brought precious cargo from the Indies, Zipangu (Japan), India, Arabia, East Africa, and as far south as the Philippines, Sumatra, Java, and Borneo. To the men of Kinsai, imperial Venice at the height of its grandeur would be no more than a backwoods village -- and Kinsai had been old in wealth and civilization when Venice was no more than a collection of mud huts. Not far from Kinsai stood the city of Sugui (Suchow), which was itself larger than Constantinople, while to the north stood the great city of Cambaluc (Beijing) from which Kublai Khan administered an empire greater than all of Europe.

For 20 years Marco Polo served Kublai Khan as ambassador, administrator and trusted lieutenant, and his work carried him to every corner of Khan's dominions. Although Marco's book described such wonders as gunpowder, cannon and compasses, it tells little of the history of the unique people who had constructed the world's mightiest civilization. If he did, who would have believed it? Who in Europe would have believed that at the time of Moses, 14 centuries before Christ, a large and prosperous kingdom (Shang) existed along the Yellow River in China whose people had mastered the arts of writing, poetry and silk weaving? Who would have believed that when Solomon built his great temple in Jerusalem 1,000 years before the advent of Christianity, the Chinese mastered the art of irrigation and, like the Assyrians, were expert in the use of war chariots? And glass -- that Venetian specialty -- would the citizens of Venice have believed it had been invented in China 1,000 years before Marco Polo's journey? Would a cultured European of the 13th century have believed that when Socrates drank his poison, Chinese philosophers already understood the properties and nature of magnetism; that while Rome battled Carthage for control of the Mediterranean, Chinese engineers completed a Great Wall nearly 1,500 miles long to defend their northwestern frontiers; that when the great library at Jerusalem was burned by the Romans and the Essenes were hiding their Dead Sea scrolls, the Chinese had their classic age of poetry and literature; that when the Emperor Charlemagne was learning to read and write, the Chinese read printed books and government employees were being graded through civil service examinations??

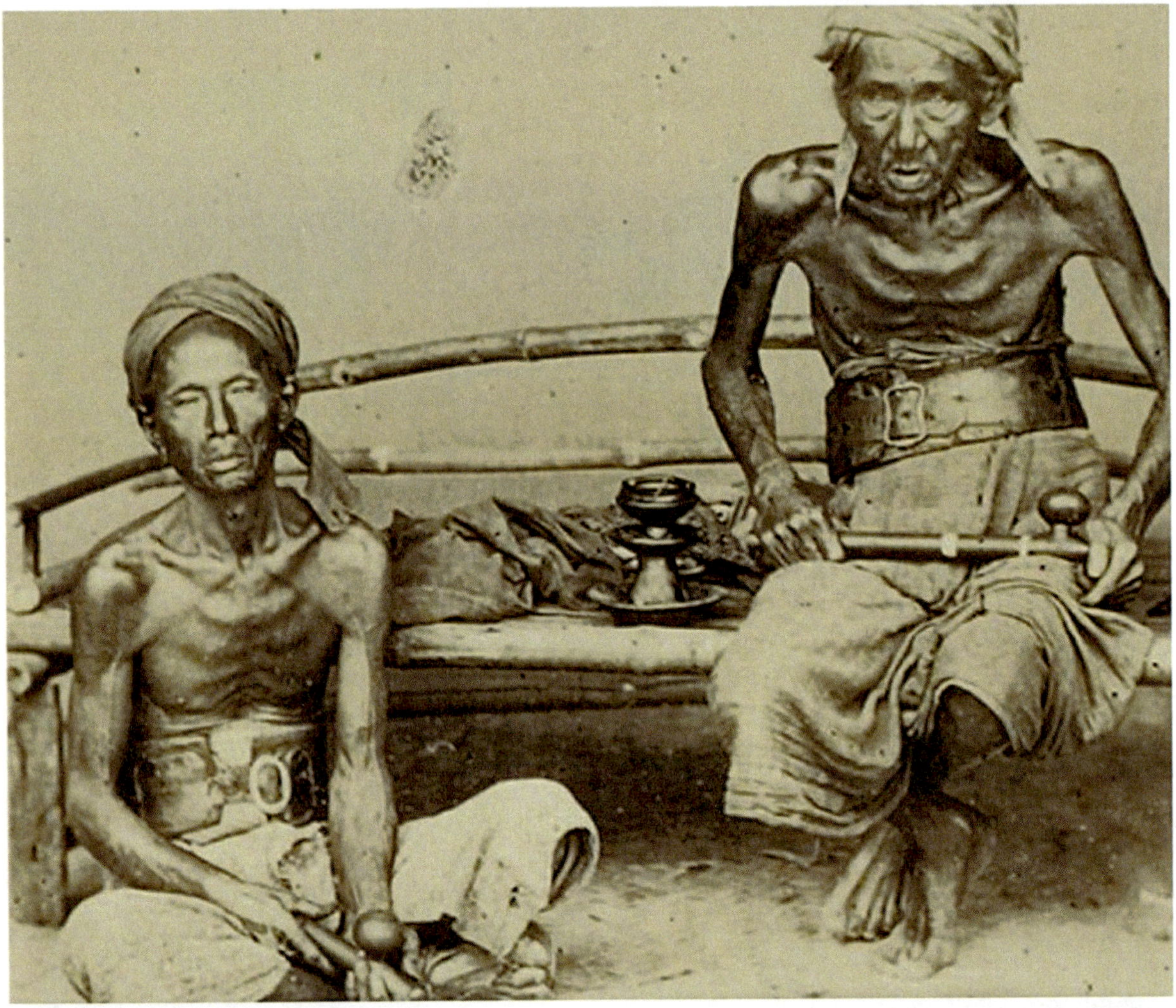

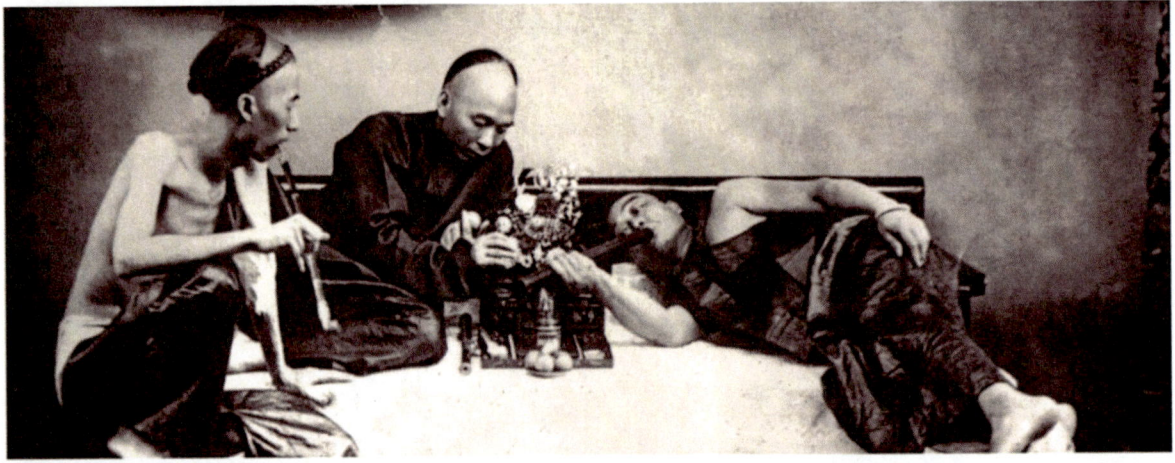

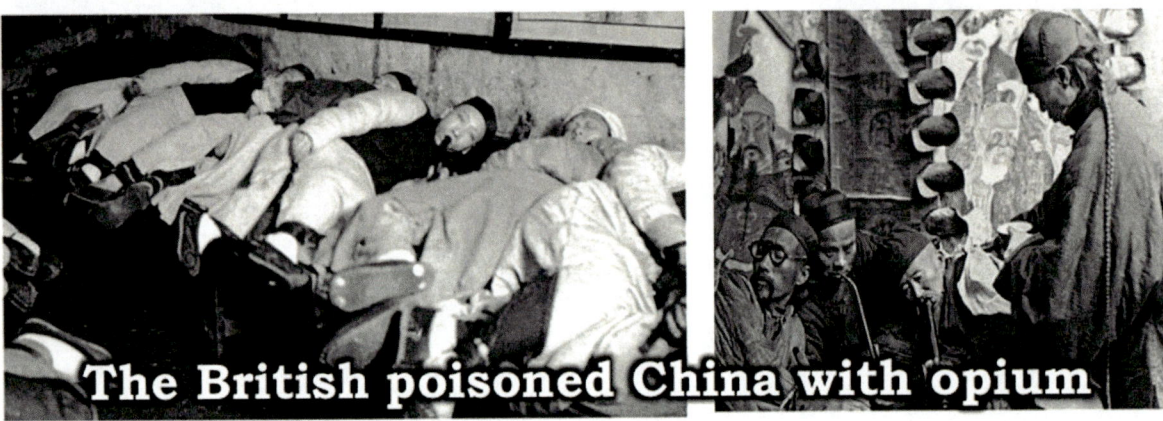

The British poisoned China with opium

Throughout its 4,000 years of history, China had no colonies, never set up military bases outside of its borders, never imposed its religion on other peoples. It endured successive assaults of Mongols, Tartars and other barbarians from the north, but were never subdued, because the Chinese did more than fight back, they wisely civilized their enemies, and absorbed them into a tolerant and superior civilization. Throughout its 4,000 years of history, China stood in splendid isolation, protected in the west by the great deserts, in the south by the Himalayas, in the east by the stormy seas, in the north by the Great Wall. Only in the last 200 years was it forced to have contact with the West. The Chinese had an infinitely superior civilization and really had very little to buy from Western merchants. In a letter to King George III of England, the Chinese Emperor remarked, "We possess all things and have no use for your country's manufactures." But if China needed little from the West, Western merchants needed much from China: silks, porcelain, glass, jewelries of magnificent workmanship, and many other luxuries wanted in barbarian Europe. How to pay for all these? The Americans arrived in clipper ships from New England laden with furs and ginseng root (valued as an aphrodisiac) taken from the Columbia River Indians, and silver dollars from Mexico. The British were more villainous. They brought opium from India into China, bribed its officials and profited enormously from Chinese addiction to the drug. From India and China the British bastards got the capital for their industrial revolution. The Chinese forbade the import of opium and burned British stocks of the drug. The British infantry landed at Tinghai, and the British cruiser *Nemesis* sailed up the Yangtze River and bombarded the coastal cities. The unequal struggle ended with the Treaty of Nanking in 1842, by which the Chinese were forced to pay for the opium they burned as well as for the cost of the war. Just as the Americans want us to pay for immoral loans they extended to Marcos, and the Low Intensity Conflict (LIC) bloodbath to kill its enemies here.

In 1853 the English and French took over the Customs in Shanghai, and opened China to a flood of Western goods which destroyed native Chinese industries. The same policy of Import Liberalization imposed upon us by the IMF and Americans. The Chinese formerly limited Western trade only to the port of Canton but the Treaty of Nanking opened other ports, and Hong Kong was ceded to the British till 1997. In Shanghai and Amoy, Westerners including Americans maintained Settlements where their own laws prevailed, and where dogs and Chinese were not allowed in parks. Chinese slave labor were imported by the British to build Singapore, and by the Americans to build the Union Pacific Railroad in the West. The humiliation and exploitation of the gentle Chinese by the Americans, Europeans and Japanese resulted in the Taiping and Boxer Rebellions which were suppressed with more cruel impositions on the Chinese people. Then in 1911, came Double Ten Revolution of Sun Yat-sen, that ended the Ancient Civilization of China that co-existed with Egypt, Rome, Greece, and outlasted them all.

If one reads the history of China, one is struck by the observation that it is "remote, obscure, and worst of all there is entirely too much of it." Chinese history overmatches that of any other nation for profusion of detail, confusion of names and sheer mass. The second salient fact of Chinese history is that far and away it is the longest continuous history of any nation on earth, reaching back to 2,000 years before Christ. The third most important fact of Chinese history has been its isolation: until the last two centuries, China has had but little contact with the outside world, and almost none with the West. For this isolation there are obvious geographical reasons. China's western land frontiers -- the great deserts of central Asia and the tremendous mountain ranges of the Pamirs and the Himalayas -- were an effective barrier to all but the hardiest explorers and traders.

Zheng He's ship compared to Christopher Columbus'

Zheng He, Emperor of the Seas

The Fleet of Zheng He

Chinese ships, once the best in the world from the 11th to the 15th century, faced by the typhoon-ridden and tempestuous China Sea and the seemingly endless Pacific Ocean to the east, turned south to the Indies and west to India and Africa.

Six centuries ago a towering eunuch named Zheng He commanded the Ming dynasty's fleet of immense trading vessels on expeditions raging as far away as Africa. Viewed from rocky outcropping of Dondra Head at the southernmost tip of Sri Lanka, the first sighting of the Ming fleet is a massive shadow on the horizon. As the shadow rises, it breaks into a cloud of tautly ribbed sails, aflame in the tropical sun. With relentless determination, the cloud draws ever closer, and in its fiery embrace an enormous city appears. A floating city, like nothing the world has ever seen before. No warning could have prepared officials, soldiers, or the thunderstruck peasants who stand atop Dondra Head for the scene that unfolded below them. Stretched across miles of the Indian Ocean in terrifying majesty is the armada of Zheng He, admiral of the imperial Ming navy.

600 years ago, almost a century before Christopher Columbus's arrival in America and Vasco de Gama's in India, the great Ming Armada weighed anchor in Nanjing, on the first of seven epic voyages as far west as Africa. All the ships of Columbus and Vasco de Gama combined could have been stored on a single deck of a single ship in the fleet that set sail under Zheng He. Zheng commanded expeditionary voyages to Southeast Asia, South Asia, Western Asia, and East Africa from 1405 to 1433. His larger ships stretched 120 meters in length (Columbus's Santa Maria, for comparison, was 26 meters). These carried hundreds of sailors on four tiers of decks. Zheng He was appointed to head the massive fleet of 317 junks (more than twice the 130 vessels of the Spanish Armada), crewed by over 27,000 men (the Spanish Armada had only 8,000 sailors). Very tall, around 6' 6", with "a voice as loud as a huge bell," Zheng He looms as a larger-than-life figure in modern eyes both in China and abroad. Yet, the authorities BURNED ALL his ships on the ground it was too expensive to maintain, and because it was said, that the Chinese is not in the business of bullying or subjugating any other people. Confucian scholars made serious attempts to expunge the memory of the great eunuch admiral and his voyages from history in the decades following his death.

As the average Filipino is nicknamed Juan de la Cruz, so is the average Chinese called Lao Pai Hsing or "Old Hundred Names" -- in reference to the 100 families who founded China many thousand years ago. Far from being one of a nameless crowd, the average man in China is accorded the dignity of an aristocratic ancestry. Till recently that is all the dignity he can claim. Old Hundred Names total more than one billion people, 20 percent of the human race. His yearly increase in population alone is more than the entire population of Taiwan. For centuries, caught between the oppressive landlord and a tyrannical government, Old Hundred Names' life was centered around his family and village, blighted by the depredations of local bandits, brutal press gangs of the army, the calculated robbery of the tax collector, and soon enough the savagery of Western colonial troops. Napoleon called China the Sleeping Giant of the East, "Let China sleep," he said, "When it awakes, the world will shake with fear and trembling."

To 19th century Western eyes, the customs of Mr. Old Hundred Names seemed a complete reversal of the natural order: **(1)** China appeared a topsy-turvy land in which the black arrows of compasses pointed south instead of north. **(2)** Old Hundred Names kept his hat on in company instead taking it off. **(3)** His books opened at the end and read from right to left vertically, instead of opening at the beginning and reading from left to right horizontally.

> **"Choose a job you love, and you will never have to work a day in your life."**
>
> — Confucius

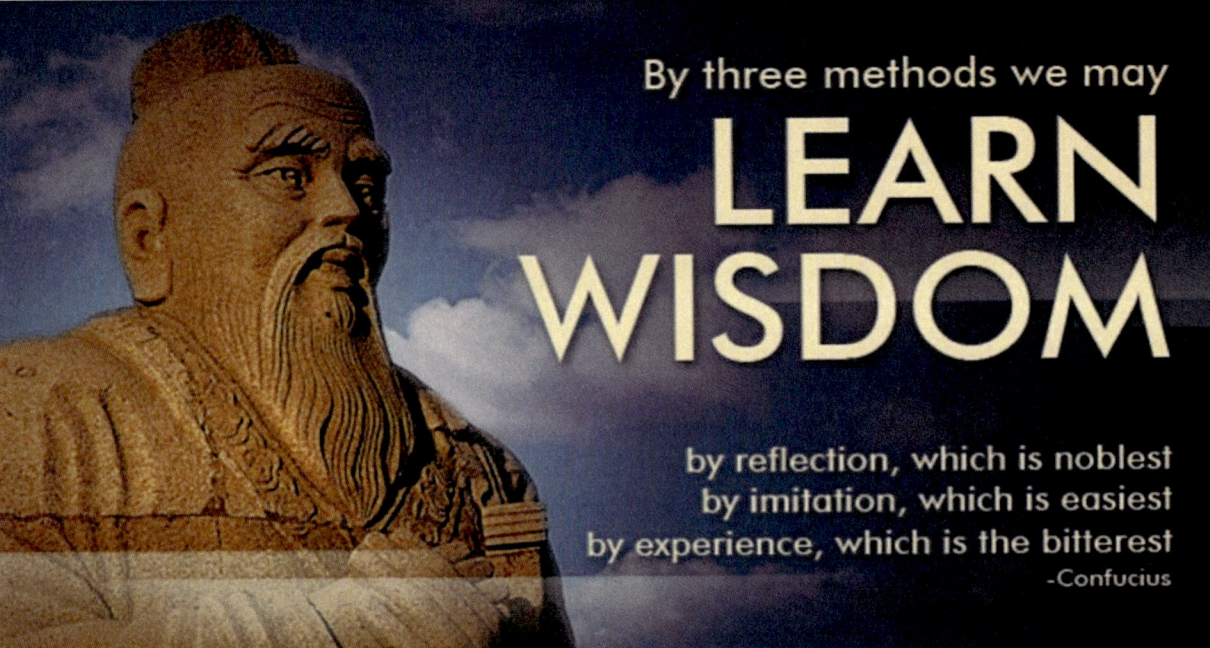

By three methods we may
LEARN
WISDOM

by reflection, which is noblest
by imitation, which is easiest
by experience, which is the bitterest
-Confucius

TOP **7** WISE QUOTES BY CONFUCIUS

1. "Everything has its beauty but not everyone sees it."

2. "Our greatest glory is not in never falling, but in getting up every time we do."

3. "What the superior man seeks is in himself; what the small man seeks is in others."

4. "Learning without thought is labor lost; thought without learning is perilous."

5. "The superior man is modest in his speech, but exceeds in his actions."

6. "What you do not want done to yourself, do not do to others."

7. "When you know a thing, to hold that you know it; and when you do not know a thing, to allow that you do not know it - this is knowledge."

"If you think in terms of a year, plant a seed; if in terms of ten years, plant trees; if in terms of 100 years, teach the people."

Confucius

It does not matter how slowly you go so long as you do not stop.

— Confucius

(4) He began his meals with desert and finished them with soup. **(5)** He placed his guests of honor on his left rather than his right. **(6)** He wore white as a sign of mourning instead of black. **(7)** He drank his wine hot rather than cool. **(8)** He brought the needle to the thread instead of the thread to the needle. **(9)** In China, the Devil was so stupid you could outwit him by merely placing a screen in front of your door; in the West the Devil was a master of cunning. **(10)** In China a written contract was considered a discourteous lack of confidence in a man's given word. **(11)** In China a girl was married in scarlet rather than in white. **(12)** In China funerals are extremely noisy affairs instead of solemnly silent occasions.

Wherever a Chinese community exists in the world, Confucius is there in spirit, even when those who inherit and transmit his mores are not quite sure just exactly who he was. In the ninth month of her pregnancy, 2,540 years ago, a unicorn appeared before Confucius' mother. From its mouth protruded a jade tablet, and on it was inscribed: "A star will descend from heaven to revive the great dynasty." Days later, Confucius' mother labored up Ni Mountain. There she delivered an extraordinarily ugly child, one with cross-eyed asymmetrical face. So grotesque was the face she beheld that she was certain she gave birth to a monster. She laid it down and prepared to abandon it. But behold, a tigress came to suckle the baby and a great eagle to fan the infant gently with its wings. Impressed by these acts of devotion, Confucius' mother swaddled the new-born baby and took it home. The boy-child was named Kong Zhongni but was always known as Master Kong or Confucius. That myth and miracle should surround the circumstances of his birth -- or any other part of a life that was governed always by reason and rationality -- would have appalled the Master, for never was a sage more certain of his mortality. It is difficult to exaggerate the immense impact that this man had on Chinese perceptions of propriety, convention and worth, or to overstate the extraordinary influence of his creed on the surrounding quasi-Sinitic cultures of Asia. Confucianism has come to stand for a philosophy of governance, a system of ethics, an emphasis on protocol and a theory of education. It has taken credit for China's stability and civil-service structure; and took the blame for what was called its pervasive and paralyzing conservatism.

In the beginning God created the heavens and the earth

Genesis 1:1

Adam & Eve mourning Abel

The torment of Job

Abraham offering Isaac as a sacrifice

David and Goliath

The Rise of Judaism

The voice of Judaism can be heard in one sentence: *"Shema Yisrael Adonoi Elohenu Adonoi Echod"* – Hear, O Israel, the Lord our God, the Lord is One! Uttered by Moses to the Jewish people, it is the prayer uttered by every Jew every morning and every evening of his life. It is the prayer he learns as a child and the last prayer he utters before he dies.

These tremendous words mark a startling departure from established religions of the past, for they created a new concept of God, One God, Monotheism, a new concept of divine and human order. Because of this, the Jews became the object of universal condemnation that led to their ejection, dispersal and Diaspora.

Theories of racial superiority tend to be discredited nowadays, but I do believe modern Jews possess certain qualities of mind and character which enable them to make full use of their opportunities, the so-called genius of the race. How did they get that way? Perhaps it could be explained by the Darwinian theories of Natural Selection and Survival of the Fittest. Two thousand years of pogroms and persecutions probably killed off the weakest and most stupid of the Jews, and left the strongest, the best, and the brightest to fill the gene pool.

It is hard to believe that Jews and Arabs belong to the same race, they are both Semites, different from the Caucasian whites. Dr. Farrukh Saleem, a Muslim, wrote: "There are only 14 million Jews in the world…. For every single Jew in the world there are 100 Muslims. Yet, Jews are a hundred times more powerful than all the Muslims put together." Then he enumerated a few Jews whose intellectual output has enriched humanity: Jesus Christ, Albert Einstein, Sigmund Freud, Paul Samuelson, Milton Friedman, Henry Kissinger, Alan Greenspan, Madeleine Albright, Benjamin Rubin (vaccinating needle), Jonas Salk (first polio vaccine), Albert Sabin (improved live polio vaccine), Gertrude Elion (leukemia fighting drug), Baruch Blumberg (vaccination for Hepatitis B), Paul Ehrlich (treatment for syphilis), – including 180 Nobel Prize winners. There are more, but we stop right here, we are convinced.

But why were the Jews so disliked by the Egyptians and the Romans? Hollywood which was founded and dominated by Jews, gives us the answers. Such movies as *The Ten Commandments* and *Land of the Pharaohs*, assert that the Jews were so brilliant that they built the Pyramids for the Egyptians. Such movies as *Ben-Hur, Quo Vadis* and the original *King of Kings,* assert that the Jews were a free people under the tyranny of the Roman emperors. Those assertions are far from the Truth. The Jews under Egypt were not the geniuses they are today, they were still a pathetic subject race, still unweeded, a tribe wandering in the Arab desert wastes. The Romans who ejected the Jews ran a civilized and orderly society based on Roman law and Roman justice, who never did what the Jews did to women (stone them when they exercised sexual freedom) and whose gods never did what the Jewish God Yahweh did: ordered Abraham to show his devotion by killing his son Isaac; allowed Job's daughters to seduce him, and tormented Job himself on a bet with the devil; massacred innocent Egyptian children; flagrantly played favorites by making the Jews his Chosen People; struck Onan stone-dead for spilling his sperms while cohabiting with his sister-in-law; turned homosexuals into pillars of salt; drowned the entire human race in favor of Noah's family and a menagerie of animals. Crazy.

Romans expelling the Jews

Hitler's Holocaust

Modern Israel

So why did the Egyptians and the Romans eject the uncivilized Jews? Most probably, when the ancient peoples politely offered to allow the Jews to contribute Yahweh to the common pantheon of ancient gods and join their body politic, the Jews insulted and repelled them with these words: "There is only One God, and we are his Chosen People. All of you are destined for hell!" If you were an ancient Egyptian or Roman, how would you react? Surely you would answer, "You arrogant pieces of dung, how dare you speak to us, your masters, in that manner? You are nothing more than disturbers of the peace, subversives of public order. You should be ejected from civilized society!" And they were, ejected, dispersed and sent on to their Diaspora, weeded by 20 centuries of persecution, and forced to be the super-race they are today.

For two thousand years, they were the Wandering Jews, a people without a country, uprooted and tempest-tossed. They became British Jews, Polish Jews, Italian Jews --- no matter where they went, they were shunned and rejected by those to whom they desperately offered their allegiance. They became isolated individuals whose existence was bounded by birth and death, and whose only concern was Self. As a result, they were driven to desperate self-seeking, a vicious, greedy, selfish, miserly people, as the rest of the world pictured them --- as Shakespeare's Shylock demanding his pound of flesh; as Charles Dicken's Fagin, teaching children how to cheat and steal.

Christian Germany once welcomed the Jews and treated them better than others. Jews spoke Yiddish, which sounds like German, had Germanized names like Goldberg, and gave their loyalty to their gracious hosts. Then in November 2, 1917, during World War I when Germany under Kaiser Wilhelm II and Great Britain were locked in mortal combat, the British Foreign Secretary Arthur James Balfour wrote a letter to Baron Rothschild, promising a national home for the Jews in Palestine. It was an empty promise that was never kept, but it appealed to Jews of the Zionist Movement all over the world including Germany. A year later, the Germans lost the war, and felt betrayed by the Jews. And it was their hatred of the Jews that Adolf Hitler exploited to unite the Germans, rearm them and, goose-stepped them towards World War II.

During World War II, six million Jews were massacred. After the War, the survivors wanted the home in Palestine once promised to them. The British and the Arabs sought to exclude 600,000 Jews from Palestine, but they forgot one thing. The Wandering Jews of Europe were isolated individuals without a sense of nationhood. But the Jews who found themselves in Palestine were no longer isolated individuals. They were an ancient people come home to an ancient land, trying to revive the shattered dreams of two thousand wandering years. And the Jews in Palestine, with a renewed sense of Nationalism, beat the British, and beat the Arabs again and again and again --2,000 years after they were ejected by the Romans, the Jews were at last back in Palestine.

The World War III has been described as the war that will end Civilization. Pope Francis now calls the war against terrorism as the beginning of World War III. The war against terrorism is a holy war, a jihad of Islam fundamentalists against the Civilization itself, with the Jews in the middle of it. The real beginning of that war was the expulsion of the Jews from Palestine by the Romans in the first century; and the beginning of the end is the return of the Jews in Palestine in the 20th century. The World War I was mostly fought in Europe; World War II was fought in Europe and Asia but not in the North and South America. But World War III spares no country and no city in the entire world. It has already begun, the great war between the Judaism, Christianity and Islam, the War that will end the world as we know it.

Romans feeding the Christians to the lions

Paul on the road to Damascus

Emperor Constantine

The Rise of Christianity

Like the Jews, Christians were also persecuted by Ancient Rome, and probably for the same reason: they refused to contribute Christ to the common pantheon on Mount Olympus, and insulted and repulsed them with the same arrogance: "We worship the One True God, and you infidels are all going to hell!" The Romans are a civilized, patient and forbearing people, and it is on record that they issued special permits to Jews and Christians to practice their religion. Do you think that Jews and Christians were grateful? Most probably they expected these gracious concessions as their inherent right, and we imagine that the Roman patience began to wear thin. The Jews were an exclusive society limited only to people of their race. As a result they were comparatively few, and easily expelled from their home in Palestine and from the Roman Empire.

The Christians were different, they were inclusive, and they converted many Gentiles and Romans to their faith. They were fanatic and persistent, welcomed martyrdom, and grew to such numbers that Romans could not safely deport them. Emperor Nero accused them of burning Rome, as an excuse to feed them to the lions and get rid of them once and for all. It did not work, they kept multiplying like rabbits on a diet of durian (a Filipino fruit considered an aphrodisiac). And when the time came, they were able to convert even the Emperor to the Christian faith.

Constantine, the first Roman Emperor to become a Christian, not only legalized his new religion throughout the Roman Empire, but sometime between 315 and 325 AD, he gave to the See of Rome (i.e., the Pope) spiritual dominion over the entire world and secular authority over Europe. He did this in a 3,000-word document called *Constitutum Constantini*, Donation of Constantine.

It was then that the Donation of Constantine was cited by various popes throughout the Middle Ages and used to buttress many of the Church's temporal claims. So influential were the popes of Rome that Popes could call upon Christian Kings to come to their aid; one of them was Charlemagne; in gratitude the Pope crowned him the Emperor of the Holy Roman Empire, under the spiritual guidance of the See of Rome, by virtue of *Constitutum Constantini*. The Church reached the height of its power in the 13th century. It had supreme authority in the field of religion, had charge of all education since the clergy were the most learned men of Europe, had large estates and great wealth, and had its own law courts to try offenders. In those days, heresy was worse than treason, because while treason was a crime against the king, heresy was a crime against God. To crush heresy, Pope Innocent III organized the Holy Inquisition. The See of Rome instituted Latin as the *lingua franca* of the western world, introduced the study of liberal arts, and established the first great universities. Civilization flourished by authority of Constantine's Donation.

The first doubts about the authenticity of *Constitutum Constantini* were cast in the 15th century. It had come to light that Constantine had given the Church of Rome authority over his capital city, called New Rome, then Constantinople, now Istanbul, at least ten years before the city even existed. By the 18th century, Voltaire could openly call the Donation of Constantine "that boldest and most magnificent forgery." The perpetrator of this atrocity has never been identified. But whoever he is, we owe him recognition as one of the greatest movers of history. Indeed, for sheer audacity and widespread effect over the centuries, this forgery has no equal. To this the greatest practical joke in all history, do we owe the supremacy of the Catholic Church in the Christian world. The 2nd Millennium, dominated by Christianity which grew to be its LARGEST RELIGION, was host to many movements.

The Crusades

Martin Luther nailing his Theses on the Cathedral door

Age of Discovery

The Renaissance in Venice

The Holy Inquisition guarded the purity of the Faith, suppressing all the heresies that arose with military precision, torturing and torching heretics at the stake, ravaging their bodies to save their souls, as they did to Joan of Arc in May 30, 1431.

The Crusades spanning almost 200 years from 1096 to 1291 AD, sent European Christian armies to wrest Jerusalem from the Arab Muslims; during that period, 9 Crusades were fought: in the First Crusade, the Christians captured Antioch and Jerusalem; in the Second, Christians lost Edessa and Damascus; in the Third, Richard the Lionheart and Saladin faced each other in an epic battle at Arsuf, which Richard won, and both signed a peace treaty; Crusaders sacking Jerusalem, smashed the skulls of Muslim babies against walls, massacred the population of 40,000, then walked on their knees on Via Dolorosa, following our Lord's footsteps to his Crucifixion; God must have been so angry that he sent the Black Death plague to decimate 25 million, ¼ of Europe's population; at the end of the Crusades, the Christians lost Jerusalem anyway. What a waste!

The Protestant Reformation started with the 1517 publication of Martin Luther's "95 Theses," calling for end to church corruption, and touting the Bible as the sole source of truth. Its ending can be placed anywhere from the 1555 Peace of Augsburg, which allowed for the coexistence of Catholicism and Lutheranism in Germany, to the 1648 Treaty of Westphalia, which ended the Thirty Years' War. The disruption triggered wars, persecutions and the so-called Counter-Reformation, the Catholic Church's delayed but forceful response to the Protestants.

The Renaissance from the 14th to the 17th centuries saw the rebirth of the pleasure loving spirit that looked back to ancient Greece and Rome. It was a time of creative genius in writing, sculpture, painting, architecture; of Marco Polo's travels to fabulous Cathay that sparked men's drive into the Age of Discovery.

The Age of Discovery seeking sea routes to Cathay and sources of spice, allowed white men to colonize other lands, convert colored people to the Christian faith with the cross and the sword, enslave the blacks, commit genocide on aborigines and steal their gold, and saw the rise of two empires upon which the sun never set: Spain and Great Britain. Finally, Western civilization intersected with Ancient China – with the Europeans deliberately poisoning the poor Chinese with opium, bullying them with gunboat diplomacy and spitting on the pride of a great people. The Japanese had their own Father-directed religion, that of the Emperor-God Hirohito, and the Sun god from which they descended, and they joined in the rape of China, and the war that followed.

The age of science and the Industrial Revolution, which promised a better life for all, resulted instead in the exploitation of the working class by Capitalist greed, and the Socialist Revolution that promised to end that exploitation, instead metamorphosed into the Communist tyranny.

The white men of Christian faith were the most terrible pestilence ever visited on mankind. With their weapons of mass destruction and a whole world to conquer, they caused more suffering on more people on earth than all the ancient peoples did – Egypt, Greece, Rome, China – and both the Jews and the Muslims, together all combined. The sonamabitches have a lot to answer for to God on Judgment Day.

Muslim desert forces from Arabia conquering Syria, Egypt, Persia

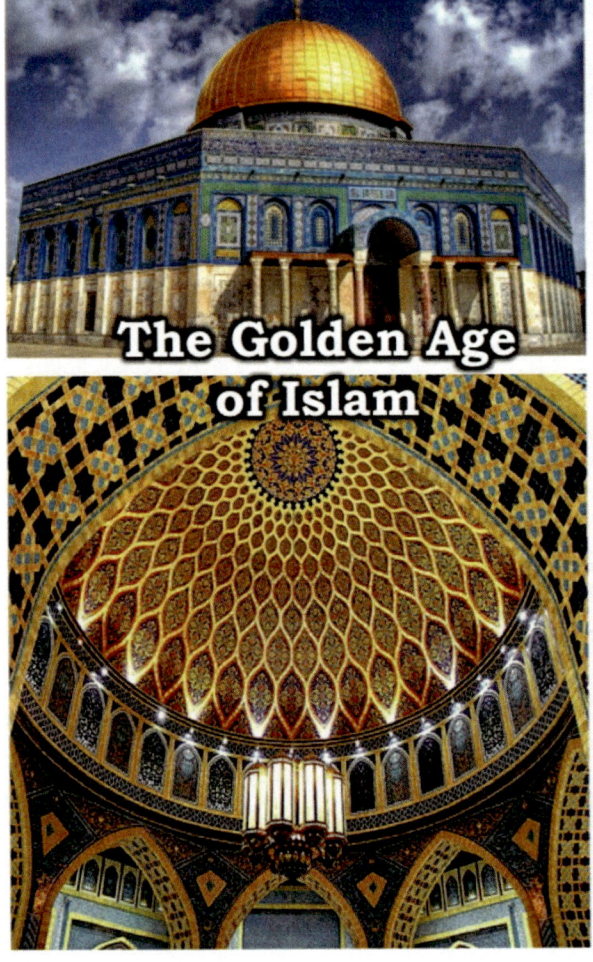

The Golden Age of Islam

Omar Khayam's Rubaiyat

The Rise of Islam

Islam, the youngest of man's great universal religions, is also in many ways the simplest and most explicit. Allah, the One God, same one as the Yahweh of the Jews, and the God the Father of the Christians, is the one true God, and Mohammed, not Moses or Jesus, is his greatest prophet. Islam came into being, not from obscure and legendary origins, but in the full light of history, with an appeal that unlike that of Christianity, is simple, lucid and affirmative. It is more than a religion, it is an all-pervasive way of life, guiding every thought and action, so that life, faith and politics are inseparable. Unlike Christianity which is split into thousands of sects, Islam is mainly divided into only two sects, the Shiites and the Sunnis, which differ not in doctrine but in the choice of the leader.

With its unclouded unity and with the zeal and martial skills of its armies under Abubakar, Omar and Osman, Islam spread with hurricane speed. One year after Mohammed's death in 632 AD, the forces of Islam burst out of the Arabian Peninsula into an astonished world ignorant of their existence. Within two decades, Islam captured all the rich nations of the entire Middle East, Syria in 635 AD, Iraq in 637, Palestine in 640, Egypt in 644 and in 650 the entire Persian Empire. So swiftly did Islam's onrushing armies advanced that in the beginning they had time neither to convert or govern their new domains. They contented themselves with exacting tribute, granting tolerance to all who paid it. Yet, in ever-growing numbers, hordes of their conquered subjects embraced the new dynamic faith that have come upon them from the desert wastes. And within one century their momentum of conquest carried the Arabs eastward to India and the Himalayas, and westward through North Africa across the Straits of Gibraltar into Spain, Portugal and France. At last in 732 AD, in one of the most decisive battles in history, they were halted by the Franks in Tours, France.

Yet the energies of Islam were not yet spent. In the 9th, 10th, and 11th centuries, while the West was mired in the Dark Ages, Islam enjoyed its golden age. By exposure to Greco-Roman, Byzantine and Persian heritage, Islam evolved a brilliant culture of its own. Art, philosophy, and poetry (*Rubaiyat* of Omar Khayyam) flourished in Baghdad. Mathematics (the arabic numerals and the concept of zero), architecture of castles and spires, and medicine advanced. Arab merchants and wandering mystics spread across Asia to Malaya, Philippines and Indonesia, and without firing a shot, and converted Malayans to Islam. Its adherents, 300 million of them, comprise one seventh of the world's population. In the broadest sense, Islam is a brotherhood of men under God, transcending the barriers of race and nation, united in an organized effort to execute the will of God. Unlike the Christians, plagued with racial and religious prejudice, cruel exploitation and colonialism, Islam looms as a religious monolith welded together by the binding force of the faith. From Morocco to Malacca, Muslims profess the same beliefs, utter the same prayers, turn their eyes toward the same holy city of Mecca. It is these things that make Islam, for all its diverse millions, the true Kingdom of God on earth.

That was before the Western corporations discovered oil in Arabian lands, and plotted to get control of it. The United States, Britain, France, and others supported dictatorships and monarchies, even overthrowing democracies, the reasons given being the promotion of "freedom", "stability", "containing the Soviet Union" and so on. This is not true of course, not for the Arabs who had their popular leaders overthrown and replaced with corrupt rulers.

The overthrow of Mossadegh in Iran

The Shah of Iran

Ayatollah Ruhollah Khomeini

One of the best known covert actions of the American Central Intelligence Agency (CIA) was its role in the 1953 overthrow of the Iranian government headed by Mohammad Mossadegh and the subsequent installation of the Shah Mohammad Reza Pahlavi into power. The Iranian Revolution of 1979 led to the overthrow of the Shah Dynasty and its eventual replacement with a National Republic under the Ayatollah Khomeini, the leader of the revolution, supported by various leftist and Islamist organizations and Iranian student movements.

It is very sad that despite their rich natural resources, the Muslims are the poorest and the neediest people in the world. The Muslim countries relied heavily on the Western countries' yearly financial aids to help them. But why all of this?! Well, the answer is quite simple. It is the lack of Islamic Democracy and Leadership in those countries. The Muslim world is either controlled by secular Muslims or extremely fanatic ones. There are no real moderate Muslims in control. There is no real Islam that serves everyone. All we have in 90% of the Muslim countries are dictatorships supported by the Western countries.

By having dictators who are nothing but puppets for the West, would enable the West to sell as much expensive weapons as possible to the "third world" Muslim and other non-Muslim countries, keeping them in a poor financial situation, minimizing any independence movement against the West, and keeping Western corporations and economies very rich. By having those dictators, it became much easier for the Western countries to politically control them.

The Saudi Arabia Kingdom today is ruled by one family. This family controls all of the country's oil resources and revenues. They literally have 100s of billions of dollars in their Western bank accounts, while most of the Saudi citizens are very poor. Now, suppose the Saudi people were able to drive out the ruling family and create a democracy where the people determine their own destinies freely. Suppose the Saudis tell the Americans, "Go away, we won't sell you any of our oil as long as you support Israel." Do you know what will happen next? The American F-16 and Stealth bombers will immediately blow away all of the oil fields in Saudi Arabia. Why would the USA do that? It's because the dictatorship that it was supporting was defeated and now the US interests are considerably influenced by another nation. This nation might not want to sell their oil for as cheap as the US used to get it from its puppets.

That's exactly what's happening to the rest of the Muslim world. Take Iraq as another example. Saddam Hussein was America's best friend and most of his weapons came from the US during the Iran-Iraq 8-year war. After he finished his war with the Iranians and decided to have a conflict with the US interests in the Persian Gulf Region, the United States was swift to beat the living hell out of Iraq in the Persian Gulf War, twice! The United States didn't mind Saddam Hussein being a butcher and a dictator before the Persian Gulf War to his people. The minute Saddam decided to violate the US interests, the US turned against him.

The trouble is when the Americans get rid of dictators they cannot control, they replace them with "democratic" governments so corrupt and so weak that they are immediately replaced by radical Muslim fanatics even harder to control, like Al-Qaeda, the Taliban and ISIS, who are conducting a holy war or jihad against the entire Western world especially Israel, against their own people who collaborate with the West. Radical Islam's holy war sets the stage for World War III that will truly be a world-wide war, targeting any city and any country in the entire planet, a war that will involve the religions of the Jews, Christians and Muslims, exactly as the Bible predicted.

End Days: Four Horsemen of the Apocalypse

CHRISTOPHER LEE
DOUGLAS WILMER
HEINZ DRACHE
and
MARIE VERSINI

in Sax Rohmer's
THE BRIDES OF FU MANCHU

The movies of Dr. Fu Manchu

Armageddon and the end of the world

According to the Bible, the end days of the world will revolve around the re-established state of Israel, after 2,000 years of the Diaspora. There will be a threat from a league headed by a great Northern nation, presumably Russia, poised to attack Israel. Israel will join forces with a ten-nation consortium of the West, probably the Atlantic Pact nations or the European Economic Community. These ten western nations are to be led by a benevolent leader (Donald Trump?), who will be assassinated and miraculously survive, leading people to believe that he may be the re-incarnation of Christ. Then there will come from the East a huge army of Chinese and Indians, also moving toward the Middle East to join the Muslims. There will be a great battle where God will destroy the Soviet Union, killing "83 percent" of the Russian soldiers. The benevolent leader of the West will turn out to be Anti-Christ, who will enter the restored Temple of Jerusalem and demand veneration. Israel will resist. Then Christ will return to earth with an army of saints and defeat the army of the Anti-Christ at the Battle of Armageddon, north of Jerusalem. The Jews of Israel will at last accept Christ as their savior. A thousand years of peace will ensue until the day of the Last Judgment, when Christ will come to judge the living and the dead.

One of the most scary possibilities, in these days of born-again Christians, not only here but all over the United States, is that American leaders will start to believe this biblical scenario and assume that this generation will see Armageddon and the end of the world. If they do, as President Reagan once believed, that the Soviet Union is really an "Evil Empire," and that the United States is fighting God's own enemies, then there is no moral justification for peace. If the Biblical Battle of Armageddon is at hand, then any search for peace is futile since God Himself is planning a nuclear war. On one occasion in 1980, Reagan was known to have said, "We may be the generation that sees Armageddon," and to have discussed with fundamentalist friends as Reverend Jerry Falwell and singer Pat Boone, such prophecies in Hal Lindsey's best-seller, "The Late Great Planet Earth." Jerry Falwell, self-styled leader of The Moral Majority who came to endorse the martial law regime of President Marcos, once said in an interview with the Los Angeles Times that Armageddon is "at that time when I believe that there will be some nuclear holocaust on this earth ... It could be 50 years. (But) I don't think we have that long." Pat Robertson of the 700 Club, an avowed candidate for the presidency of the United States, said practically the same thing.

There is no scriptural basis for the American role at Armageddon, so that it can not be presumed that a U.S.-Russian war will fulfill any biblical prophecy. Hal Lindsey wrote a new book "The 1980s: Countdown to Armageddon," in which he urged the United States to maintain an aggressive nuclear stance. Since God Himself will destroy his enemies at Armageddon, no one need fear that a superpower will beat Him to the punch. But a strong national defense ensures a safe America for Christians till the moment God decides to rescue them out of danger.

It is amusing to note that Americans as a rule always consider themselves the good guys while all the rest are the bad guys. In movies of the exotic, mysterious and inscrutable East, we hiss the warlords of China, the fanatic soldiers of Japan, and such characters as Doctor Fu Manchu. Then there are the historical sagas that depict the cruel and despotic Spaniards as arch villains. Then the usual anti-Nazi and anti-Communist villains, who are exactly the same except for the names, all of them depicted as contemptuous of democracy, and totally devoid of human compassion. Lastly, the Terrorists most of whom are Negroes, Arabs and lunatics.

Muslims worshipping the Black Stone

Christians worshipping at the Vatican City

Jews worshipping at the synagogue

Sophisticates assume that villainy need not be limited only to America's enemies. Many movies depict American multinational companies and American robber barons as possible Anti-Christ, depicted in St. John's vision in Chapter 13 of the Revelations: "A Strange Creature ... with seven heads and ten horns, and ten crowns upon its horns ... requiring everyone to be tattooed with its mark, so that no one could get a job or even buy in a store without the permit of that mark ... with the Devil's power to fight against God's people and to overcome them, and to rule over all nations and language groups throughout the world." No better description of transnational corporations with their trademarks, concentration of economic power, and power to subvert and corrupt nations, can be found.

How startling it is to realize that Biblical Prophesy mirrors Reality. In the course of human affairs, we have seen the rise of Ancient Religions which lasted for millenniums, for thousands of years, under religions that are family oriented and mother-directed, only to be replaced by three father-directed alpha-male religions that are self-destructive, which in 20 turbulent centuries are ushering humanity to the edge of extinction. These religions of the Jews, Christians and Muslims are the same cast of characters that we find in the Biblical prophesy of Armageddon and the end of the world. I refuse to believe that our extinction is pre-destined. We must achieve what Toynbee calls the "synthesis of all faiths" and go back to earlier times when there was a multiplicity of gods, family oriented and mother-directed, living together in peace in a common pantheon, without bigotry or discrimination, and with Tolerance, Goodwill and Compassion above all else.

Endless are the ways that man worships, ranging from the horrible to the sublime to the ridiculous -- proof that whatever else he may be, Man is a religious being -- the only creature, according anthropologist William Howells, "who comprehends things he cannot see and believes in things he cannot comprehend." Most living religions assume that they come directly from the hand of God, unique like the biblical Melchizedek, "without father, without mother, without descent, having neither beginning of days, nor end of life." But that is not so. Religions have their genealogies, they are born, they live and they die, like any human institution.

We tend to mock the unfamiliar in other faiths, by labeling them idolatry or superstition. We hurl such words at others, rarely at ourselves. Yet every man commands respect at the moment he bows his head before his god. At that moment of prayer every man is at his best, and if we are wise, we shall try to understand and appreciate his faith. Arnold Toynbee repeats the increasingly familiar refrain that all religions are but different paths to the same God, and hopes for a synthesis, a "syncretism" of all faiths: "The four higher religions are four variations on the same theme. If all the four components of this heavenly music of the spheres could be audible on Earth simultaneously, and with equal clarity, to one pair of human ears, the happy hearer would find himself listening, not to a discord, but to a harmony."

In their religions, men do not really differ. They seek the favor of their gods, protection from danger, community with their fellows, courage in the hour of conflict, comfort in the hour of grief, guidance in their daily concerns, and some hope for immortality. Salvation comes only when, in the words of the prophet Micah, our faith inspires us "to do justly, to love mercy, and to walk humbly with God."

People at Marian Shrine in Lourdes

People at Marian Shrine in Fatima

Breastfeeding Madonna

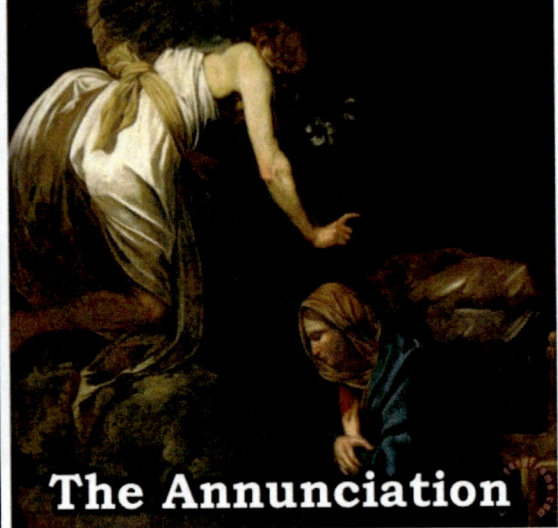
The Annunciation

Mary, the greatest celebrity of all time

So little is written in the Bible about Mary, and only in the Gospels of Luke and Matthew and they did not even use the term "virgin birth." Neither Mark nor John wrote of her in their Gospels. Later Mary appeared with men said to be brothers of Jesus. Taken literally, this belies the claim that she was a virgin all her life, but her followers argue that Jesus' brothers were Joseph's children in a previous marriage, or his cousins, or objects of his brotherly love.

In the Bible, she was accorded no special honor by Jesus or his followers. She was there for the crucifixion, and was mentioned in the Book of Acts as a member of the early church in Jerusalem. St. Paul referred to Christ as "born of woman" and did not mention her name. Only at the beginning and end of the life of Jesus did she play prominent roles. Of Mary's later life, nothing is known and it is very unlikely that she participated in Jesus' ministry during his lifetime.

The cult of Mary started in the second century with a document called "Protoevangelium of St. James", which filled in the details of Mary's life, and which was never accorded canonical authority. The concept of Jesus' virgin birth was fiercely debated even then. By the fifth century, the Council of Ephesus, against much opposition, certified her virginity and called her the Mother of God. The massive split called Reformation came about partly because many Protestants could not accept two new ideas: the doctrine of Immaculate Conception that Mary was born free of Original Sin, and the doctrine of the Assumption that Mary without dying was borne bodily to heaven. Immaculate Conception became Catholic dogma in 1854, and the Assumption in 1950.

More was written in the Bible about the Magdalene and the women of the Old Testament than about the Virgin Mary. Yet the idea of the virgin Mary, so sparsely drawn and subject to many interpretations, has dominated much of last 2,000 years of religious history, alternately elevated and demoted by the Catholic Church, at one time or another shunned, attacked and praised by Protestants. The Muslims regard her as pure and holy, mentioning her 34 times in the Holy Koran and upholding her virginal conception of Jesus, and large numbers of Muslims are making pilgrimages to Marian shrines. Protestants, some of whom reject the super nature of the Virgin, miss having Mary. "I envy Catholicism its Mary" said Forrest Church, a Unitarian Minister. And Mary hymns are creeping into Methodist hymnbooks.

Even the Women's Lib claimed her for their own in their fight to achieve equality with men and priesthood for women. From being the humble and submissive handmaiden that conservative Catholics say she is when she said, "Be it done to me according to thy word," Mary is regarded by liberals as an independent woman, pointing out that God did not force a decision on her, he sent the angel Gabriel to get her consent. The choice was Mary's. "If by her own free will she had refused God -- as did Eve, the mother of man – then God's plan had to change. The entire plan of salvation hung in the balance. So if, as various interpreters have said, God does not rape, God woos, then it had to be a free and independent source of action in Mary that made this happen. This makes her not a passive receptacle," but a willful and decisive agent of destiny.

Why did Mary appear in more apparitions than her God Son? Why are there more shrines dedicated to Mary than to any other? Why is Hail Mary a more popular prayer than Our Father? Why did five million people, many of them non-Christians, visit Lourdes this year to drink its miraculous waters?

Our Lady of Medjugorje

The Nativity

Our Lady of Mexico

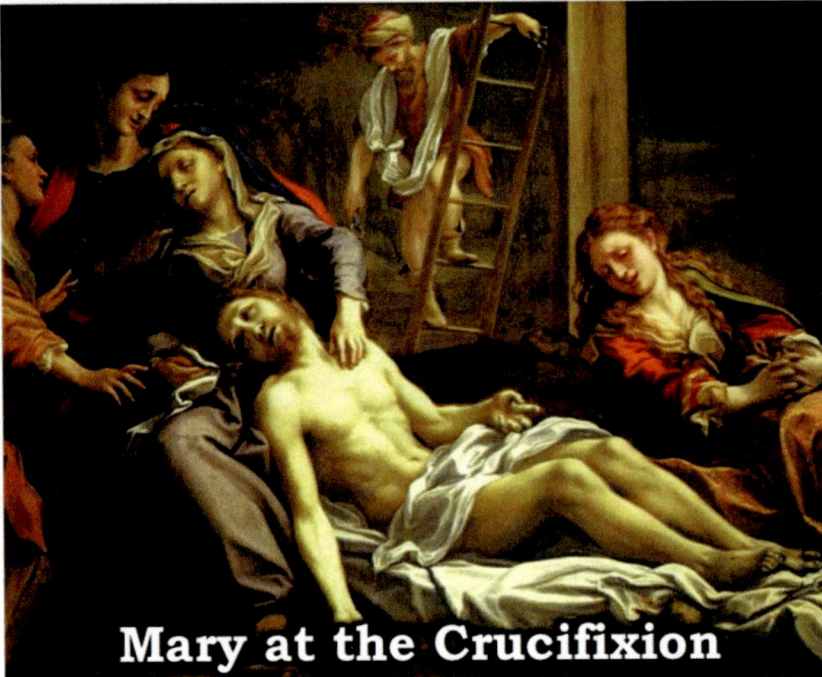

Mary at the Crucifixion

The Assumption

Why did more than 10 million people troop to Guadalupe to pray to the Virgin Mary? How come the miracle of Fatima? How come the thousands upon thousands of weeping Madonna statues all over the world? Despite the reluctance of the Church to certify to the apparitions of the Lady of the Roses at Lipa, the Lady of the Snows in Belleville, at Bayside in Queens, at Medjugorje where Bishop Pavao Zanic grew apoplectic at seeing Mary as a tourist attraction – how come Marian Tours are burgeoning as well-organized and well-attended industries? How come after the Vatican II decided to downplay Mary to appease the Protestants and pave the way for the reunification of Christendom, the cult of Mary still persists, stronger than ever before, specially among the non-Christians and Protestants too?

The answer is that Mary belongs, not to the priests, but to the people. No matter what has been decreed in a given era, the popular passion for her has remained resolute. Her disciples, Catholics and non-Catholics, have adamantly refused to let Mary fade away. For 2,000 years she has been the greatest celebrity of all time, because she is not one Mary but a thousand different Marys (Our Lady of Sorrows, of Joy, of Peace, of Love), constantly being re-invented to be relevant to every age and to every human being. The saving grace of our trying times is the emergence of Mary. Mary is the only symbol of the Female Principle in our modern world. There is nothing comparable to Mary in any other modern religion. That is why she is being revered as a Mother figure even among Protestants and Muslims, conservatives and liberals, agnostics and atheists.

Mary is all things to all men. She is at home everywhere – Our Lady of Guadalupe, of Fatima, of Lourdes, of Manaoag, of Medjugorje. She has many faces – Our Lady of the Snows, of the Elms, of the Lilies, of the Roses, of the Woods. She has many expressions: Our Lady of Sorrows, of Peace, of Adoration, of Divine Intercession, of Love, of Heavenly Joy. She represents the very best qualities of Womanhood: a Virgin who is also a Mother, not only Queen Mother but also Mother of God, and above all our very own Mother.

"There are a thousand and one Marys at work in the world today, but it can be argued that after 2,000 years we are delivered four principal Marys who seek to soothe the soul of modern man."

Each is unique, each powerful in her own way: **Miraculous Mary,** the messenger of God; **Mediator Mary**, who intercedes for us before God's judgment seat; **Modern Mary**, the symbolic leader against a male hierarchy that seems intolerant, autocratic and wholly unreasonable, who with Mary Magdalene was staunchly with Christ to the end, while the Apostles deserted him on the eve of crucifixion; and above all, **Mother Mary**, the Madonna with Child, answering to a deep emotional need and irresistible to a troubled world, an Everyman's mother, a bridge between religions, whom we all can approach for sustenance, understanding, mercy, forgiveness and unquestioning love. **Mary is perfect as symbol of the Mother Principle for our Future World.**

Mary is constantly being re-invented by people to fit their needs and circumstances, but the old definitions of her do not slip away. They accumulate, they grow, they accrue, they pile up to shape a human being of great worth to us all -- till the Mary of today becomes the Mary of the past, the future and forever.

This piece is paraphrased partly from an Internet article entitled The Mystery of Mary, which we found while surfing the internet for dirty pictures.

Queen Victoria

THE TIMES OF INDIA

INDIRA GANDHI SHOT DEAD

Sikh security men pump
bullets in chest, abdomen

Funeral on Saturday: 12-day mourning

Some of Queen Victoria's Royal Descendants:
Kaiser Wilhelm II
of Germany
Czar Nicholas II of Russia
Christian X of Denmark

Queen Elizabeth I

Queen Elizabeth II

Of Women Leaders

In the year 2001, lo and behold, we had a woman president in the person of Gloria Macapagal Arroyo who succeeded a lousy president Erap Estrada, as Cory Aquino succeeded another lousy president Ferdinand Marcos, through a people's power revolt. One must admit that elected women heads of state (as distinguished from "women behind the throne") have proven themselves the best of leaders. Ever since 1960 when Madame Sirimavo Bandaranaike of Ceylon became the world's first woman prime minister, women held their own on the world stage with the possible exception of President Isabelita Peron. Prime Minister Golda Meir of Israel, Prime Minister Indira Gandhi of India, and Prime Minister Margaret Thatcher of the United Kingdom certainly presided over what may be considered a golden age in their respective nations.

Men leaders often underestimate women leaders, always to their surprise and dismay. Half a dozen Arab leaders of 60 million Arabs thought that grandmother Golda Meir, head of 2 million Israelis, was a pushover. While the Israelis were observing their Yom Kippur, the Arabs attacked without warning; Golda's forces swiftly struck back and forced the Arabs to their knees in a lightning 11-day war. Long afterward, when Anwar Sadat of Egypt landed in Jerusalem, his old nemesis Golda Meir together with Premier Begin, was there to meet him. "Here's the lady I long wanted to meet", exclaimed Sadat. And Golda smiled her broadest smile, embraced him and answered softly, "What took you so long?"

The military leaders of Pakistan underestimated grandmother Indira Gandhi of India, and baited her into a couple of border incidents. As a result, Pakistan lost Kashmir and East Pakistan (which became the new nation of Bangladesh). Indira's political allies turned against her for exercising dictatorial powers under emergency decrees tantamount to Martial Law. She graciously called for elections, her party hopelessly splintered, and lost. The next time around, she decisively beat all her opponents and became the undisputed leader of 600 million people, the largest democracy in the world. Pakistan's President Mohammed Zia underestimated the daughter of the man he overthrew and executed, Benazir Bhutto who subsequently became the Prime Minister of Pakistan, first woman leader ever to head a Moslem nation.

The military dictators of Argentina likewise underestimated grandmotherly Margaret Thatcher of the United Kingdom of Great Britain and Northern Ireland, and made a grab for the Falkland Islands. Her nation reduced to a second class power, with the roar of the British lion down to a meow, Margaret Thatcher against all advice waged a war halfway around the world, and won. The dictators of Argentina were themselves overthrown by their own people.

Prime Minister Margaret Thatcher somehow brings to mind one of England's greatest rulers, Queen Elizabeth I, whose reign brought us the golden age of William Shakespeare, and who defied the greatest naval power of the time, Imperial Spain. The Spanish monarch, Philip II, after whom the Philippines was named, sent the greatest fleet of war vessels across the English Channel, the dreaded Spanish Armada. In a few days' battle, aided by a storm, Elizabeth's small fleet of privateers destroyed the Spanish Armada, and made England a great naval colossus and the greatest colonial power of all time.

Elizabeth I shares that distinction with Queen Victoria who ruled Great Britain for 64 glorious years, presided over the expansion of the British dominions to such magnitude that it could be

A lion and his pride

A Cock and his Chickens

Isabelita Peron

Imelda Marcos

President Corazon Aquino on Ayala Avenue

said, "The sun never sets over the British Empire." She was conferred the title Empress of India, and from her loins and her genes came forth almost all the titled heads of Europe, from the German Kaiser Wilhelm II to the Spanish King Alfonso XIII to the Russian Tsar Nicholas II.

What makes women leaders different from their male counterparts? A look at the lower animals provides part of the answer. The male of the species, from the lordly lion to the cocky rooster in the chicken coop, fights for power for one purpose, sexual dominance. He fights to copulate with the prettiest females around, and the more he deflowers and impregnates the better. The deadlier female fights too, but her sex drive is sublimated into a noble undertaking: the care and protection of her brood. Men instinctively seek power for power's sake, while Women seek power in pursuit of a primordial urge, a mother instinct that seeks to embrace a whole nation. If Indira Gandhi really wanted power for its own sake, she would never have voluntarily relinquished her dictatorial emergency powers and called for elections she was bound to lose.

Yet not all women leaders are like Indira Gandhi. President Isabelita Peron of Argentina was not. She was not elected to the Presidency. She was elected as Vice President, succeeded to office upon the death of her husband President Juan Peron, and was subsequently overthrown. The chief difference between Indira and Isabelita is their age. Like her predecessor Evita Peron, Isabelita was young, was still in the childbearing age, and had no children. Because of this, she had a compulsive need to be attractive, to be admired, to be envied, to be desired, to be courted and to be pursued. One might add, Imelda Romualdez Marcos was in the same category. Such women seek power for the beauty and luxury it affords, and they are more often than not, the power behind the throne rather than the person of power.

Women of childbearing age have an additional burden to carry, they have to contend with "monthly periods" causing a chemical imbalance that sometimes upsets Reason and Judgment. But beyond the age of childbearing, at the stage when she becomes a grandmother, a woman becomes a potential national leader with a capacity for greatness rarely achieved by the male of the species. Such women leaders are almost always underestimated by men, and almost always to their surprise, consternation and dismay. Pushed to the limit, such women leaders have proven stronger than their male counterparts.

A woman leader has a capacity for greatness rarely achieved by the male of the species. Firstly, because unlike the male, she is motivated less by the quest for power than the mother instinct to embrace and protect the entire nation. Secondly, women have to try harder and accomplish more to get the same recognition that men get. Thirdly, they are much more consummate politicians, used to persuasion rather than command, after a lifetime of cajoling dominant and philandering husbands; persuading and disciplining recalcitrant children; bargaining with vendors and peddlers; and making peace with intransigent mothers-in-law. They will have cultivated the supreme qualities of patience, understanding, and dissimulation to a degree unattainable by male politicians. Fourthly, a woman is stronger in will and healthier in body than men are. Men can hardly cope with an 8-hour day, coming home to rest in the arms of a wife who never rests. The women have to be in better shape in order to withstand the rigors of childbirth and breastfeeding, the pangs of insecurity that is the lot of most wives, the 24-hour job of being wife and mother, weathering family crisis upon crisis without let-up. She has less nervous breakdowns and less debilitating diseases than her husband, and generally survives him. In the fires of life's tribulations, the woman becomes tempered steel, better equipped to cope with crises that beset a nation.

MEN are from MARS

WOMEN are from VENUS

Live!

- Women more valuable, we send men to war.
- In a One-Man World among women, world population does not skip a beat.
- In a One-Woman World among men, we're back to Adam and Eve.
- When men become Kings, Popes, Priests, Mandarins and Supreme Court Justices, they wear a woman's gown.

Above all, a woman has the quality needed to be a great leader and manager of the affairs of the nation, because she is a generalist instead of a specialist. Anyone who ever climbs up the corporate ladder to be CEO of the company knows that the higher up one reaches, the less he practices the specialization for which he is trained. He must know about everybody's contribution to the company objective. He must be a bit of a lawyer, an engineer, an accountant, a human relations expert, in order to guide the varied specialists under his authority towards a common goal. The more responsibility he assumes, the less specialist and the more generalist he has to be. But all her life a woman is a Generalist rather than a Specialist.

To survive as a successful breadwinner, a man has to be a specialist, a lawyer, an engineer, a doctor; in short, a man has to be One Thing to everybody. On the other hand, a woman has to be Everything to somebody; she has to be a babysitter, teacher, guardian, policeman, warden, nurse, doctor, psychologist to her children; she has to be a bit of an engineer to be able to operate and fix household appliances; a bit of an accountant to plan the family finances; a bit of a lawyer to keep her family out of trouble; a bit of an artist to decorate the home; a bit of a wife and a prostitute, a bit of a chef and a courtesan to keep the interest of her husband. Even as she delegates her duties to her children and servants, she becomes to all intents and purposes, General Manager of the home. As such, she acquires the empathy, experience and judgment invaluable in exercising the leadership of a nation.

They say men are from Mars and women are from Venus. But that is only partly true, women are also from Mercury, Saturn, and from millions of planets, because women differ from each other, far more than they differ from men. Women have an extra X chromosome, so much larger than the men's tiny Y chromosome. That is why women have more choices, they wear different dresses and shoes than other women do, men prefer to wear the same pants and shoes every single day of their lives, like other men do; that is why women are so unpredictable and men are so predictable in all matters.

Women are the nurturers of the human race, they are anchor of the family, the cornerstone of civilization, and far more valuable than men who are so disposable, we send them off to wars to be killed without counting the cost. That is why we save women and children first, and save men for the very last.

Imagine a world of women with only one man. One whole country can be re-populated by one normal ejaculation of 50 million sperms by that one man. The world will not skip a beat.

Imagine a world of men with only one woman. That one woman can only give birth once every 9 months. The world will be back to the time of Adam and Eve.

Women are much much more valuable than men are. Small wonder then that when talented men attain a position of wisdom, prestige and power above ordinary men.... when they become popes, cardinals and priests, rabbis and mandarins..... when they become Supreme Court justices and Kings..... they are called upon to dignify their person with what women ordinarily wear.... a gown!

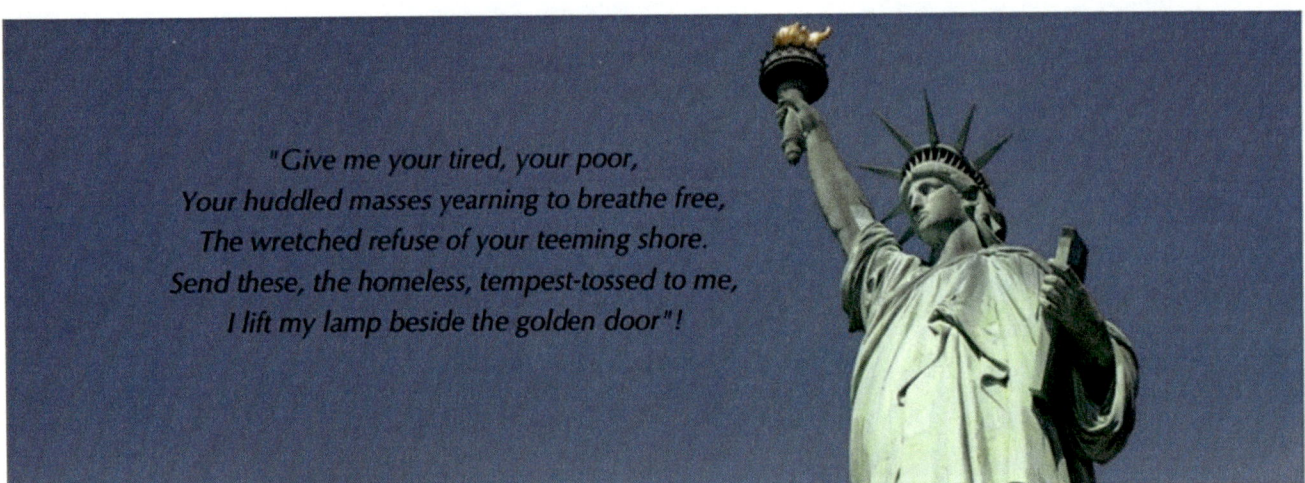

"Give me your tired, your poor,
Your huddled masses yearning to breathe free,
The wretched refuse of your teeming shore.
Send these, the homeless, tempest-tossed to me,
I lift my lamp beside the golden door"!

Dr. Vicki Belo

Jaime Laya

Raul Manglapus

Heherson Alvarez

Jose Aspiras

Benigno Aquino Jr.

Carlos P. Romulo

The First Citizens of the World!

Not like the brazen giant of Greek fame,/ Conquering men, astride from land to land,/ Here in our sea-washed sunset gate / Shall stand a mighty woman with a torch,/ Whose flame is the imprisoned lightning,/ And her name -- Mother of Exiles./ From her beacon hand glows world-wide welcome,/ Her mild eyes command the air-bridged harbor/ Between cities famed./ "Keep, ancient land, your storied pomp,"/ Cried she with silent lips,/ "Give me your tired, your poor, your huddled masses,/ Yearning to breathe free,/ The wretched refuse of your teeming shore -- Send these, the homeless, tempest-tossed, to me. I lift my lamp beside the golden door."

Certainly not like the Colossus of Rhodes is the American Statue of Liberty, which welcomed waves of poor immigrants from Ireland, Italy, Scandinavia and the rest of Europe, and less enthusiastically the "unassimilable Asiatics" like the Japanese, Chinese, Filipinos, Vietnamese and Koreans. But poet Emma Lazarus' immortal poem, quoted above, part of which was etched on the base of the statue itself, serves to remind us all that once the United States was the haven of the poor and oppressed people of this world.

Those seeking political asylum, such as Raul Manglapus, Sonny Alvarez, and Ninoy Aquino himself, always found themselves welcome in the United States. My family and I, to the chagrin of many who accuse me of being anti-American and who could not get a US visa themselves, have been going in and out of the United States and are always welcomed with unfailing courtesy. So nothing prepares us for the occasional bastard in the US Bureau of Immigration who takes pleasure in tormenting Filipinos at the port of entry. Senator Sonny Alvarez was insulted, falsely accused of a criminal act, shouted at, and detained for several hours. Former Central Bank Governor Jaime Laya was also detained and handcuffed. Also former Tourism Secretary, and former Congressman Jose Aspiras was so treated, as were three other Congressmen, and many Filipino citizens with valid visas. Even former Secretary of Foreign Affairs Carlos Romulo whose loyalty to the USA is far above his love for the Philippines, according to Anding Roces, was once shouted at by an American immigration official, "In this country you are nothing!"

I guess it had to happen to one of my family, although it most probably had nothing to do with my stand on the US bases. My daughter-in-law, Dra. Vicki Belo-Henares, is the daughter of lawyer and ex-Assemblyman Enrique Belo, who supports the American Occupation of the Baselands. Yet Vicki who travels back and forth to and from the United States several times a year, this time for a few months' training in dermatology, was detained in the Los Angeles airport sometime ago. She was accused of using a spurious and tampered passport, of having a passport picture that does not look like her, kept incommunicado for an entire eight hours, and subjected to invectives and insults: "What are you doing with an American Express card? Filipinos cannot afford to have credit cards like these. You must be an illegal immigrant!... Where did you get $5,000 in cash and travelers' checks? You stole them, admit it!... This is not your passport, your picture does not look like you at all, you tampered with this, it is probably fake!... No, you cannot make a phone call. You have no rights in this country. You have no choices except two: either turn right back and go home, in which case you will not be allowed to come back here for the next three years; or go to jail right now and rot there!... You goddamn bitch!" Torrents of tears and eight long hours later, without an explanation or apology, Vicki was released, and was allowed to go her way. Well, such is life, there will always be an asshole who likes to boast that he gave hell to someone better than he is.

Pia Wurtzbach
Miss Universe 2015

Gloria Diaz
Gloria Diaz
Miss Universe, 1969

James Younghusband
& Angel Locsin

Anne Curtis

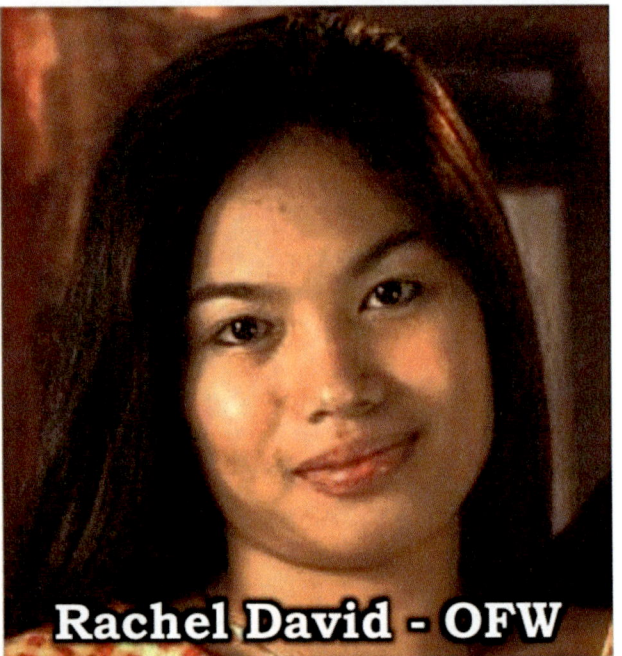

Rachel David - OFW

Boboy Garovillo

Jimmy Alapag

Maribel Ongpin

But what is really incomprehensible is the reaction of most Filipinos to such an incident, "Well it is our fault. We have no gratitude, *walang utang na loob*, we do not give the bases to the Americans, so why should they treat us with any respect? Besides, if we are allowed into the United States, chances are we will go TNT (*tago na tago*, meaning we will be illegal aliens)!" Because of our colonial mentality, because we are without a sense of pride, of dignity and of self-respect, we are treated like dirt even by other peoples. The wife of Jimmy Ongpin who is a pro-American, actor-singer Boboy Garovillo, and a Filipino Jesuit priest of French descent, were treated shabbily by Italian immigration inspectors at the border. Mrs. Puring Tamayo, wife of the Air Force General was stopped at the London airport.

I myself was kept for forty-five minutes at the Seoul airport because in my passport, some mathematical genius in the Foreign Affairs figured my height to be 152 centimeters. That made me a five-foot dwarf the size of Mayor Jojo Binay, and opened me to the charge that I was traveling with a tampered passport. What could I do? While the wheels of justice ground slow, I spent the time staring at the Korean lady immigration officer with a pretty face and big boobs, and orbited into flights of fantasy that would have done justice to Penthouse magazine. She finally became embarrassed and let me go before I was able to imagine what Filipinos call *sarap ng buhay* (the sweetness of life).

We have lost our country to the multinational corporations, to American militarists, to the CIA and the IMF. There is no more hope here so we have to go elsewhere to survive with dignity. Not even God knows, according to Foreign Secretary Raul Manglapus, how many Filipino immigrants, legal or otherwise, are in the United States, in Spain, Italy, Germany, England, Hong Kong, Singapore, Taiwan, Saudi, Kuwait, and in the rest of the world. We are the new Wandering Jews, scattered to the four winds in our Diaspora.

We are the new citizens of the world. And where our women serve as domestics, private nurses and nurse-maids in the richest homes of the world, we take care of the next generation of world leaders. Our women have the hands that rock the cradle and rule the world. Like the Jews, we will prevail.

Sometimes I wonder about my own countrymen, my fellow Filipinos. As a well-read sophisticate, I sometimes find them weird, a people conquered by the Americans in the most cruel manner, and treated like Indians and Negroes with unequal treaties and high-handed economic policies, having a "Stockholm Syndrome", a passionate love for their tormentors beyond all understanding, loving Americans more than their fellow Filipinos, and blindly loyal to the American flag over their own flag. *Onli in da Pilipins* can this happen.

But then, maybe we Filipinos must be made of different stuff from other human beings, maybe we are really aliens, because in many ways, we differ from other peoples. Most societies regard half-breeds as products of miscegenation, and treat them as outcasts of society, except *in da Pilipins*. Here we prize half-breeds or mestizos as potential beauty queens, movie stars, basketball and football players – we regard them as an improvement of our race.

Take the way we eat, for instance. We like to use our hands to eat, but we really don't have to. There is no Filipino dish that we cannot eat with a spoon and fork. On the other hand, the Americans and Europeans whom we admire so much, do eat with their hands, because they have to.

Eating with fork & spoon

Sinigang

Kare-kare

Serenade

Pinakbet

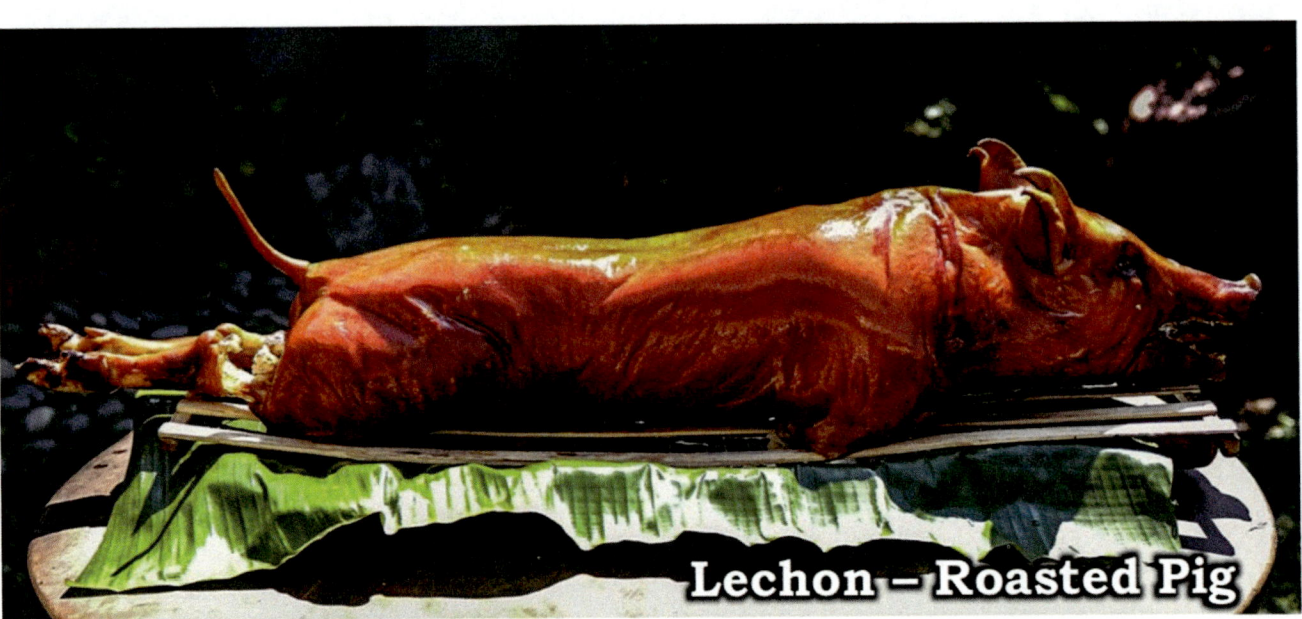

Lechon – Roasted Pig

There is no other way to eat sandwiches, or pieces of bread, or French fries, ice cream cones, or drum sticks, other than with hands and licking fingers. So do people from India and the Middle East when they take unleavened bread and wipe it on bean paste. On the other hand, Eastern civilizations influenced by the Chinese use chopsticks, a civilized way unless you are a tree hugging environmentalist. When white people use dinner-ware, they use the most inefficient way of doing so – with a fork and knife. So-called Westernized Filipinos struggle to eat peas or rice with a fork and knife, they are so pathetic! The most efficient way to bring food to your mouth is the way only Filipinos do, with a spoon and fork. The spoon is most versatile, it can be used not only to take peas, soup and rice, but also to cut the soft meat and veggies served to us, better than a fork or a chop stick. Most of our dishes are delicious and nutritious combinations of meat, vegetable and soup, to eat which all we do is to hold a fork in the left hand and a spoon on the right, no changing of ware from one hand to the other. *Onli in da Pilipins* is this done.

Our Blessed Mother, the Virgin Mary, in most pictures and statues with her Baby Jesus, seemed forever wistful, seldom bursting with motherly enthusiasm. When Mary was asked why, she answered, "Well, to tell you the truth, I was hoping it would be a girl!" It is fascinating to speculate what might have happened if Jesus had been a girl. Me, I believe in womanhood, and so does the Filipino people. In Philippine society, women occupy a position that is the most unique in the world. A female child born to a Filipino family is welcomed as a sign of good fortune, as contrasted with the female child in parts of old China who is considered a liability and is liable to get drowned at birth. In the Philippines, the sanctity of her person and of her chastity is guarded with almost fanatical zeal by grandmothers and old aunts.

And no wonder. When the time comes for her to get married, the man of her choice must prove himself worthy by offering one year's labor free to the girl's parents. He must pay large sums of money or gifts to all sorts of relatives as a token of gratitude for their having raised the girl especially for him to love. All this before the girl is even committed to marry him. When the formal engagement is announced, the man is expected to build a house for the bride, and to give her a complete wardrobe, starting from the comb in her hair progressively down to the shoes for her feet. Then when the wedding comes, the man or his family pays for all the expenses of the ceremony from the bridal gown to the wedding feast. In the rest of the world, it is the bride's family that does the paying. In other words, the Filipino man provides the wedding dowry, not the woman. And this practice is known nowhere else in the world, not in the authoritarian societies of Asia, not even in the liberal-minded nations of the West where women first won the battle for political equality.

The difference does not end there. In the United States and elsewhere, the man comes home with the paycheck, gives the household allowance to his wife and school allowances to the children, and keeps the rest in the bank in his own name. The man does the family saving and investment. It is not so in the Philippines. The Filipino comes home with the paycheck and gives it to his wife. The wife gives the children and the husband their allowances. The man is the breadwinner, and he often has to hire himself out to an office or factory to get a steady income. The woman is the keeper of the keys to the exchequer, and it is in this role that she often finds herself as an investor and risk taker. The more enterprising woman takes the family savings and goes into business -- a small store under the house, a cottage industry, or even a pawn shop. She may not always succeed, but if she does, chances are she makes more money than her husband, and finds so little time left for the family that she asks her husband to quit his job and manage the business for her. And that is how family fortunes are started -- by women.

Prince William's Filipina nanny invited to royal wedding

BY LEO REYES   APR 29, 2011 IN ENTERTAINMENT   LISTEN | PRINT

Prince William's nanny Araceli "Lillie" Piccio from Bacolod City, Philippines has received an invitation to attend the Royal Wedding of Prince William and Kate Middleton to be held on April 29 at the Westminster Abbey, United Kingdom.

The First Citizens of the World:

- Hands that rock the cradle rule the world
- Second biggest English speaking country, not white but brown
- Filipinos love America over their own country
- Ten million Filipinos in Diaspora all over the world

But the Filipino woman will never admit this, not in a manner that might rob her husband of his prerogatives as king of the manor and the lord of her creations. It is in this light that the Filipino woman plays her unique role as the traditional keeper of savings and investment, the entrepreneur and founder of family fortunes, and as the focal center of the home and Philippine society.

Only from the Philippines comes forth a Diaspora totally unlike that of the Jews. Unlike the Jews who are faced with anti-Semitism and fear of their financial and political influence, and control over the movie world, Filipino immigrants unobtrusively blend into the white society, asking no "affirmative action" to advance their cause, and serving their hosts with competence and humility as care-givers, doctors, engineers and accountants. But it is as care-givers, nurses, and *yayas* (nannies) that they are welcomed into the home of the rich and the powerful. There they nurture with love the future leaders of the world, and give meaning to the saying that "the hands that rock the cradle are the hands that rule the world." I have met and heard of many youth, like that of the British royalty, who speak Tagalog, eat *adobo*, and trek to the Philippines to invite their Filipina *yayas* to their weddings. Of all the minorities in the USA, Filipinos are most likely to become Republicans who hate the Afro-Americans and the Latinos. Why? Because most of the Filipinos never had to depend on the charity of government as most minorities do, and advanced on their own initiative and determination, as Republicans want Negroes and Latinos to do. It is hard to imagine Filipino immigrants turn fascistic against the poor, and in favor of the rich, there they are... *onli prom da Pilipins!*

All over the world, public toilets come in pairs – his and hers, male and female – but notice this, women's toilets are always crowded, men's toilets are not, because women take twice as much time to take a leak than men do. *Onli in da Pilipins*, and only in one place, the Aliw Theater of Liza Macuja and Fred Elizalde, do we have two toilets for girls for every one for boys.

Onli in da Pilipins are successful revolutions like EDSA conducted like fiestas and religious revivals. *Onli in da Pilipins* do we have women so beautiful that Filipino men worship them and send them all over the world to become beauty queens, and wives of the rich and powerful. So enamored of creatures in skirts who promise heaven on earth are the Filipino men, that they readily surrendered to white men in skirts (cassocks, garb of priests) who also promise heaven, but not of this earth. *Onli in da Pilipins* would you find a colonial people thoroughly converted to the way of life of their colonial masters. The British, the French and the Dutch conquered peoples and left them exactly as they found them, with the same religion, the same language and the same way of life. The Spaniards and the Americans did not only want to exploit us, they wanted us to be ersatz Spaniards and ersatz Americans. The Spaniards made us Catholics, the Americans made us speak English, gave us universal education, potable water and political corruption. *Onli in da Pilipins* do we have such a schizophrenic people -- an Asian people with funny Spanish names, who cannot speak Spanish; the second largest English speaking country whose people are brown, not white; *onli prom da Pilipins*, do you find a people who love the world more than their own country, and who are truly the First Citizens of the World.

Women of the Philippines have always dominated the world stage of beauty queens. Filipino citizens married the first Miss Universe Armi Kuusela of Finland (1952), and the first Miss International Stella Marquez of Columbia (1960). Subsequently, the Philippines managed to win its own 13 titles of the Big Four beauty pageants, more than any country except Venezuela: Three Miss Universe; One Miss World; Six Miss International and Three Miss Earth.

First Miss Universe
Armi Kuusela
and her Filipino husband

First Miss International
Stella Marquez and her
Filipino husband

CICELY:
THE STORY OF A DOCTOR

Cicely Williams:
"Milk and Manslaughter"

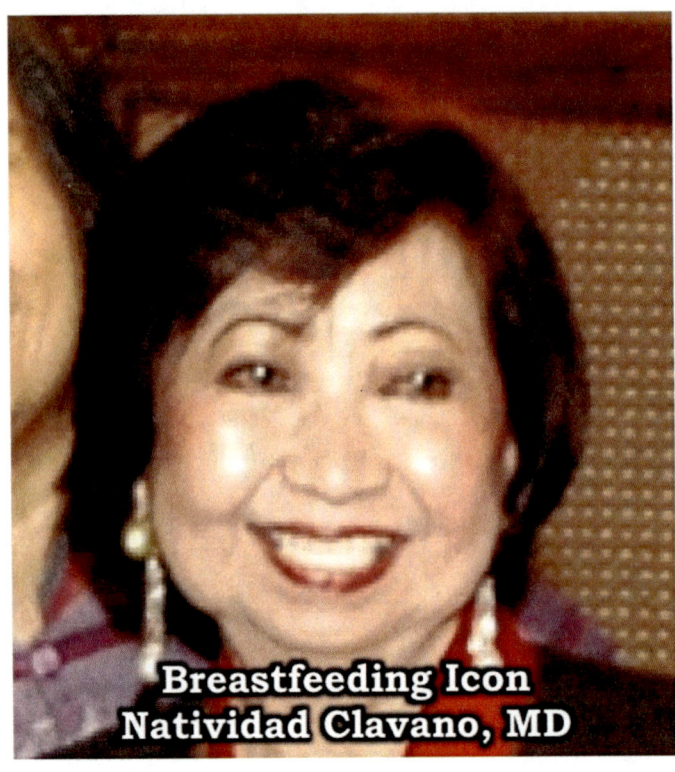

Breastfeeding Icon
Natividad Clavano, MD

Philippines' First
Nutritionist
Manuela G. Maramba

By 2016, in the the Tokyo Film Festival, the Filipino actor Paolo Ballesteros won the the first Best Actor award in a transgender role, "I thought I was up for Best Actress," he joked, joining Linda Hunt and Hillary Swank in the Best Actress category for transgender roles.

But Philippine dominance transcend beauty contests. In one particular world war, the Milk Wars, involving Nestlé and the milk companies versus breastfeeding advocates, Filipina women were prominently involved. In 1867, Henri Nestlé developed a breakthrough infant food from cow's milk, at about the time the movie industry began as the most pervasive medium in the history of the world. With the help of movies, the company founded by Nestlé almost completely eliminated breastfeeding as the norm for the nourishment of human babies; nudity censorship forced even Disney Studios to avoid breastfeeding scenes and advance bottle-feeding as the norm for nourishing babies, arousing the ire of the world's health authorities. The Milk Wars is the longest war in modern history, exceeding the bloody wars against Fascism and Communism, in duration, scope and casualties in human lives, and it still goes on today.

In 1939, **Dr. Cecily Williams**, a physician from our part of the world, working among the poor in Asia, gave a speech, "Milk and Murder," to the Singapore Rotary Club in which she said "misguided propaganda on infant feeding should be punished as the most miserable form of sedition, and these deaths should be regarded as murder...." Nestlé Kills Babies was the battle cry of breastfeeding advocates, initiating a Nestlé boycott. In 1945, the first Nutritionist in the Philippines Ms. **Manuela Maramba**, working in the Food and Agriculture Organization (FAO), objected to the UNICEF bringing in a shipment of milk into the Philippines, arguing that this would sabotage the country's breastfeeding culture, that the Philippines is not a milk producing country, and has many indigenous foods which are a better source of calcium. Miss Maramba's objection was of course disregarded by the Philippine Government due to the influence of Nestlé, the Milk Companies, and the US government.

In 1978, the US Congress was deluged with mail against Nestlé. Senator Edward Kennedy, chair of the Senate Subcommittee on Health and Scientific Research held hearings on the promotion and use of infant formula in developing countries. In these Kennedy hearings, Nestlé sent eminent doctors all over the world, to speak up for the infant milk formula. Then one little Filipina lady, **Dr. Natividad Clavano** of Baguio General Hospital of the Philippines came by her lonesome to testify on a monumental study she made involving 10,000 babies over a period of five years, absolutely banning bottle-feeding, that resulted in 98% reduction in infant diarrhea and 96% reduction in infant mortality. What a sensation she was! And calling attention to Nestlé's unethical marketing practices, Senator Kennedy called on the World Health Organization (WHO) to "do something about this!"

The following year, 1979, WHO and UNICEF hosted an international meeting and called for the development of an international code of formula milk marketing. In 1981, the International Code of Marketing of Breastmilk Substitutes was adopted by the World Health Assembly (WHA) by 118 votes to 1. The LONE dissenting vote was cast by the United States due to pressure from its Milk Industry. This was followed by another WHO/UNICEF treatise on the "Global Strategy on Infant and Young Child Feeding in 2002."

Five years later, in 1986, following a revolution that ousted the Dictator Ferdinand Marcos, the first Woman President of the Philippines **Corazon Aquino** issued Executive Order 51 (EO 51) adopting in full the provisions of the WHO/UNICEF International Code of Marketing of Breastmilk Substitutes.

Filipino Women Presidents:
Corazon Aquino and Gloria Macapagal-Arroyo

Aquino proclaimed Executive Order 51, a law that protects breastfeeding and Arroyo instituted its Implementing Rules and Regulations.

Breastfeeding pioneers:

Ines Fernandez

International Board Certified Lactation Consultants:
Elvira L. Henares-Esguerra, MD
and Nona D. Andaya-Castillo

Filipino Flag RED up:
At war with Milk Companies, Corporate Draculas and the US Government

Filipino Flag BLUE up:
at peace with WHO, UNICEF, Department of Health and Mothers of the World

But the first Implementing Rules and Regulations (IRR) issued "temporary exemptions" to all the Milk Companies pending the shift of policy towards the Breastfeeding Culture. For the next 20 years, 11 versions of the revised IRR were drafted by the Department of Health, and rejected again and again by The Inter-Agency Committee where the milk companies were represented, while a lone breastfeeding organization **Arugaan** headed by Ms. **Ines Fernandez** fought a lonely and vain battle, against Nestlé and the American Embassy.

Then two more breastfeeding advocates joined the crusade against the milk companies, a dermatologist/pharmacist/mother Dr. **Elvira L. Henares-Esguerra,** and an activist/mass communication graduate/vegan Ms. **Nona Andaya-Castillo**. In 2005, Elvira who is my daughter, came to me in tears because she was told by the Department of Health that she cannot attend a public hearing on Breastfeeding, because there is no room for her. Me, I was 81 years old at the time, and engineer from the Massachussetts Institute of Technology, a doctor of economics, a former cabinet member as Chairman of the National Economic Council, a former President of the Chamber of Industries, columnist and a radio and TV commentator, and a pretty grouchy old man with a penchant for mouthing expletives. How do you think I would react at the tears of my daughter? I burst into the public hearing, berated government officials for their cozy relationships with the enemies of breastfeeding, called the representatives of the milk companies agents of Western Colonialism, and swore that the 12th version of the breastfeeding rules and regulations will be the last, and will be passed into effect if I have to bring it to the President of the Philippines myself.

At that time, the breastfeeding issue was considered nothing but gender issue, something most people make fun of. We made it a universal rights issue by establishing two tipping points: Breastfeeding is the most wide-spread and least costly strategy for the alleviation of poverty; and Breastfeeding provides the Social Capital for the lifetime health, emotional stability and intellectual development for the future citizens of the world. We attacked the enemy at ten points of intervention for the promotion, protection and support of breastfeeding, from getting Educational Authorities to introduce breastfeeding in all health subjects at all levels of schooling, to getting rid of nudity censorship that look upon bare breasts as sex objects rather than instruments for the nourishment of future generation (we got Cardinal Vidal to approve the bare breast display of the Virgin Mary, followed by approval of the same by the Vatican Press).

We unfurled our Philippine Flag RED SIDE up, saying we were at war with Milk Companies, the Drug companies, the Tobacco companies, all foreign Corporate Draculas and Imperialist America, and inverted the Flag BLUE SIDE up to indicate we are at peace with all patriotic Filipinos and forged a coalition with President Gloria Arroyo (the Second Woman President of our country), Health Secretary Francisco Duque, Undersecretary Alexander Padilla – the so-called Pangasinan Mafia, for we were all from the same province – together with Unicef Country Head Nicolas Alipui. We eventually got a petition signed by 100% of the Catholic Bishops, the mainstream Protestants, the Buddhist Community, 20 out of 23 Senators, 1/3 of the most influential Congressmen, to have the new IRR approved. To get newspaper headlines, we had the President issue a Presidential Proclamation to celebrate the World Breastfeeding Week on August 1 to 7 every year at Malacañang Palace, we earned the Guinness World Records for single-site breastfeeding, for multiple-site breastfeeding, and for most trees planted, we organized a Synchronized World Wide Breastfeeding at local time for all the 24 time zones, organized a Breastfeeding Olympics in China and brought home the only Gold Medals (two from WABA, a third one given to a Chinese police woman who breastfed earthquake survivors).

Breastfeeding Antagonist
Senator Pia Cayetano
with Nestle connection

Breastfeeding Champion
Congresswoman
Anna York Bondoc

Breastfeeding Antagonists:
President Benigno
Aquino III, Health
Secretary Enrique
Ona

Breastfeeding Superstars:
Health Secretary
Francisco Duque,
Unicef Chief
Nicolas Alipui,
PhliHealth Head
Alexander Padilla

We got the offices of US senators Charles Schumer, Barbara Boxer, Barack Obama and Hillary Clinton to help us with a case of official corruption at the Department of Justice, against Wyeth International for selling 4 million cans of contaminated milk in the Philippines. We won our fight in the Executive Department by having the Revised RIRR for EO 51, signed by the Secretary of Health in 2006, in the Judiciary, by winning the fight at the Supreme Court challenging its constitutionality in 2007, and had Congresswomen **Anna York Bondoc** file a bill to institutionalize it into law in Legislature, had it passed by the Lower House in 2008, and narrowly missed passing it in the Senate *sine die* session, through the machinations of a woman senator, **Senator Pia Cayetano** who was Chair of the Senate Committee on Health, with close ties with Nestlé.

Dr. Elvira L. Henares-Esguerra was appointed by President Gloria Arroyo Special Envoy to convey the highest Presidential Awards to Senator Edward Kennedy posthumously, to Dr. Natividad Clavano, to Ms. Manuela Maramba, and to Unicef Executive Nicolas Alipui, for their roles in advancing the Breastfeeding Movement in the Philippines.

This Breastfeeding Movement in the Philippines is the MOST successful in the entire world, and a beacon to all nations of the Third World. In this revised IRR, the milk companies are forbidden to give gifts, travel grants, research grants to any doctor or health official, any pregnant or nursing mothers; are forbidden to advertise formula milk for babies up to two years of age. There is only one thing which we regret, it was not passed into law, and therefore subject to amendments by future presidents. The next President Benigno C. Aquino III, the bachelor president who plays video games, dates women, drives fast cars and goes target shooting with high powered guns, something that my sons already abandoned at the age of 16, did not continue with the official celebration of World Breastfeeding Day. He caused the Chief Justice of the Supreme Court, to be impeached and dismissed for hiding his true assets, and caused 3 senators to be indicted for plunder by the Ombudsman. But he also appointed a Secretary of Health who was dismissed for corruption. Before he was fired, the Secretary entered into a Memorandum of Understanding with Pfizer Corporation (which at the time bought out the Wyeth International who makes formula milk), indicted for Corruption by the US Justice Department and the SEC, and fined $2.5 Billion for violations of the Foreign Corruption Act; and then he loosened a little the IRR to allow milk Companies to advertise formula milk for the first year of the baby's birth. Because of Senator Pia Cayetano, we failed to impose heavy penalties for violation of EO 51, as directed by the Supreme Court. The Milk Wars go on, and we already won most of the battles.

For sheer determination, brilliance of strategy, and broadness of vision, the women of the Philippines have proven themselves without peer as citizens of the world.
My daughter Rosanna delivered this "TED TALK" in November 2016.: *I am not a hero. I am merely a breastmilk broker. Some people are real estate brokers, or stock brokers. I broker for breastmilk. My name is Rosanna Henares Angeles and I started the Angels Breastmilk Bank for the Premature. My story involves a lot of heroic acts, of people who acted outside of their own interests in order to do something kind. That is to me, a hero. My husband and I did not marry early, he was 30 and I was 29. So, we wanted to have children immediately. All I ever wanted to be was a mother. But year after year, we miscarried. We had a total of five miscarriages. Five babies lost. Five times our hearts were broken.*

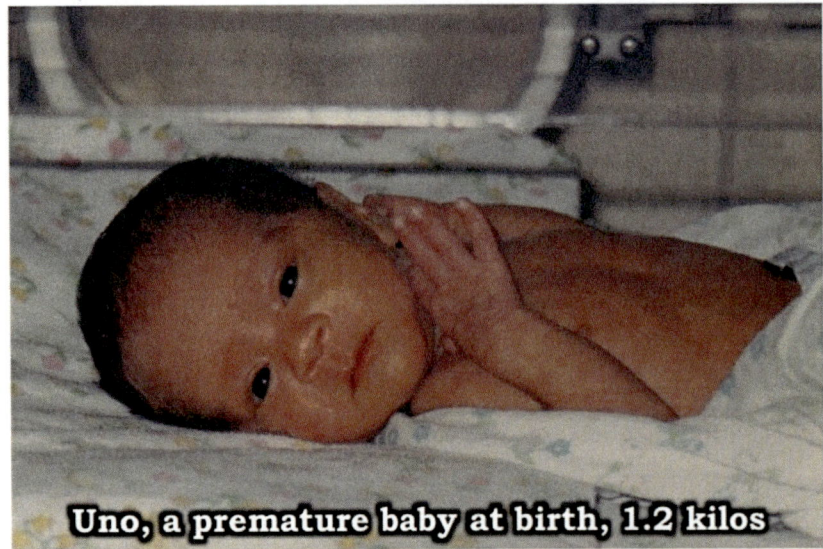

Uno, a premature baby at birth, 1.2 kilos

Rosanna is the Founder of the Angels' Breastmilk Bank for premature babies that saved more than 500 lives.

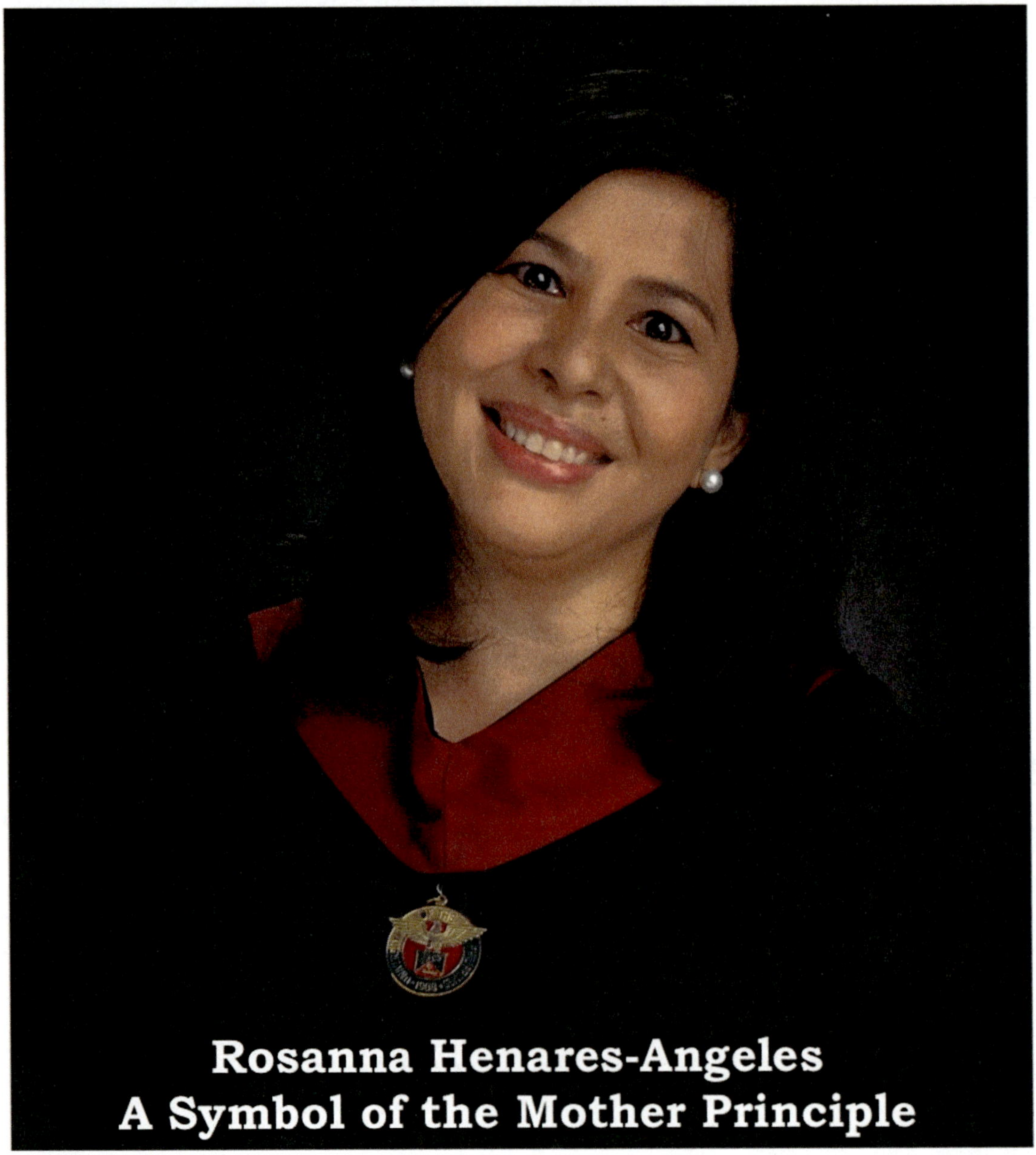

**Rosanna Henares-Angeles
A Symbol of the Mother Principle**

I had what you call a reproductive immune disorder. The problem was not in getting pregnant, but in nurturing the baby to full term. Our doctor said that the only way we could have a child was to follow a rigid medical protocol blood: thinning injections every day, progesterone injections every other day, ultrasounds every week, intravenous immunoglobulin every month, and many other things I don't care to remember. Yet all our doctors warned, that this was all experimental and that ultimately, our journey may end in wounded hearts. Despite all this, our fifth pregnancy still ended in a miscarriage. Through ultrasound, we saw our fifth child die little by little, her heart beating slower and slower, until after 11 days at the hospital, the beating finally stopped. At this point, my husband said, "We've been asking God repeatedly for a child, what if His answer was NO?" I never thought of that. And just as I had succumbed to this possibility. God surprised us and finally said YES. On November 11, 2001, after 7 years and 5 miscarriages, Uno was born. We were overjoyed. We asked and we asked and we asked, and finally...we received. We still had our challenges. Uno was born severely premature. Uno weighed all of 1.2 kilos. If you had ever bought a kilo of rice or a kilo of sugar, well, my son weighed roughly that. He was placed in the Neonatal Intensive Care Unit or the NICU, but we were assured he was fine and that they were only waiting for him to grow. I looked at his incubator and thought, "Wow, after 7 years, I am finally a mother. He looked at me. He recognized my voice, my song, and I was eternally connected with this tiny being. Then, right before my eyes, he turned black. Not blue, but black. Sensing something was wrong, I quickly alerted the nurses and watched as the whole NICU was a blur of activity. Nurses checked his vital signs. The supervisor called the neonatologist. A priest came to hold my hand and asked if he could baptize this boy who might very soon lose his life. One moment he was fine, then the next moment he had sepsis, a life-threatening infection of the blood. The doctor said, "To be honest, we are not sure Uno will make it. We will do all that is medically possible to keep him alive. For now, go home and pump for breastmilk. It is the antibiotic that may save your child."

I went home hoping Uno would survive the night. I was trying to, but pumping breastmilk when your child is at the brink of death is not an easy task. My cousin's wife took pity and gave me some spare breastmilk. She was saving this milk for her own child, but she acted out of kindness and gave them to Uno. She was to me, a hero. She gave 12 four-ounce bags. At that time, you couldn't buy breastmilk. I guarded them with my life. The 12 bags were to be consumed in 3 days. When I was down to my last two bags, the doctor said, "I know Uno is still at the Intensive Care Unit, but can you give your last 2 bags to Ysa?" Ysa was in the next incubator, Uno's first neighbor. Ysa, One in our language as Uno is One in Spanish. Ysa weighed 600 grams, imagine, half the size of my already tiny Uno. My reaction was "NO way! Do you know how hard it was to find a breastmilk donor? Let them find their own donor!" But then my husband and I stepped back and realized, that this milk was given to us out of kindness, so sharing our last 2 bags with Ysa, whose issues were even worse than Uno's, was the right thing to do, even if we had no idea what Uno would be drinking in the morning. But see, here's the twist. Within one hour of sharing the milk, one hour, a grade school classmate of mine, someone I had not seen nor talked to for 25 years, called...out of the blue. I don't even know where she got my number. She said she had just given birth and heard I was pregnant. I said, "I gave birth prematurely. Would you have extra breastmilk?" Her reaction was larger than life. "Oh my gosh, yes!" "I just let it go down the drain but my breasts, you better believe it, these tiny breasts, can fill a lake!!!" One hour...that's all it took. One act of kindness. Imagine...just 2 bags of milk and I was given a lake!!!

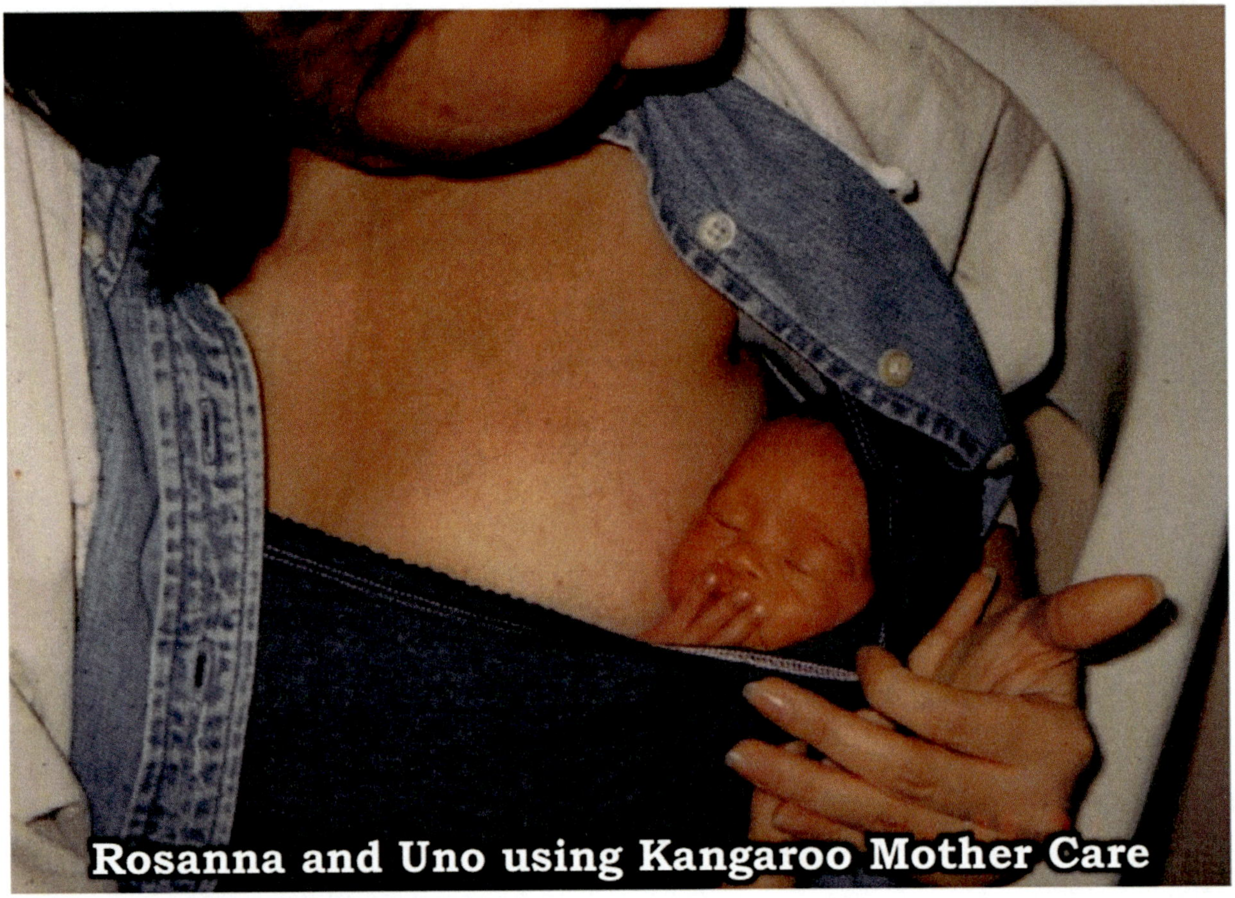

Rosanna and Uno using Kangaroo Mother Care

Angeles Family with Larry Henares
Rosanna, Uno, Vigo and Husband Eric

This friend made pumping breastmilk a career. She hardly ever pumped breastmilk before. She found it inconvenient, having to sterilize the bottles and buy plastic bags. She just fed her children directly from her breast. But, she pumped breastmilk for Uno. Not only at night but several times throughout the day. Her kindness led her to action and she was to me, a hero. After that, donor after donor came. Remember that this was in 2001, with no social media. But donor after donor came, generous souls that pumped the night away to give Uno their extra milk. All these mothers had nothing to gain by giving us their breastmilk. In fact they lost sleep in doing so. But all of them said that giving made them feel good. I received so much human milk that I started the Angels Breastmilk Bank to pay it forward and to help other mothers like me.

And this is the point I am making today. We hear so much of hatred nowadays. Corruption. Drugs. Extrajudicial killings. Hate crimes. People say it's an epidemic. But, if hatred can grow wild, KINDNESS can go viral. We need kindness, now more than ever. My son Uno is now 15 years old. Take note, this was the picture he approved for this presentation. And this is him with his 12 year old brother Vigo. Countless of mothers have since donated to the Angels Breastmilk Bank. Powered by these mothers' kindness and volunteering spirit, we have, in 15 years, helped at least 500 premature infants on the brink of death. Free of charge. Just mothers helping mothers. Mothers who have more, helping mothers who have less.

Using the milk God had placed near their hearts to heal and nurture not only their own child, but a child who may, like Uno, need it to survive the night. Now... these are your everyday heroes! Real heroes who through their kind acts, make the life of other human beings better. You see... you can like kindness. You can share kindness. Kindness can go viral. Let me give you some examples that you as college students can do. A friend of mine, a graduate of this school, committed to sponsoring birthday parties for children with leukemia, every quarter of every year. She wanted them to celebrate their lives. She used to do this by herself but then her kindness had caught on and now many people donate to her cause. Another friend, in an effort to cheer up a friend with cancer, ambushed Jericho Rosales and made him hold a sign saying "Laban Pilar." Her kind act spread like wildfire. Friends, acquaintances, even people who hardly knew her, rallied and asked celebrities to hold up that Laban sign. These pictures were not photoshopped. Celebrities like Kyra Sedgwick, Dustin Hoffmann, our own Derek Ramsey, Sen. Pacquiao, Pres. P-Noy and now even athletes from opposing teams have gotten together, to wish her well and to encourage her to endure and continue her fight against cancer. We wanted the same girl to know how much we loved her. So we, her high school classmates from Batch 82 began 82 Days of Christmas. From October 5 till Christmas day, she has and will receive a letter and a gift from 82 friends. Kindness HAS ALREADY gone viral. After giving their gifts, people felt so good that they asked if they can be given another day. It turns out, this is no longer just a gift for Pilar, it has become, really, a gift for ourselves. Much like my breastmilk donors who said if felt so good to give. Miraculously, and this is how kindness works, the givers have become the receivers. The givers have become the receivers. You see kindness CAN spread... not only outward, but within. So, throw your kind act into the universe. Make kindness go viral... and allow the spark to begin with you. Remember only one thing. It isn't always easy but Always Choose Kindness.

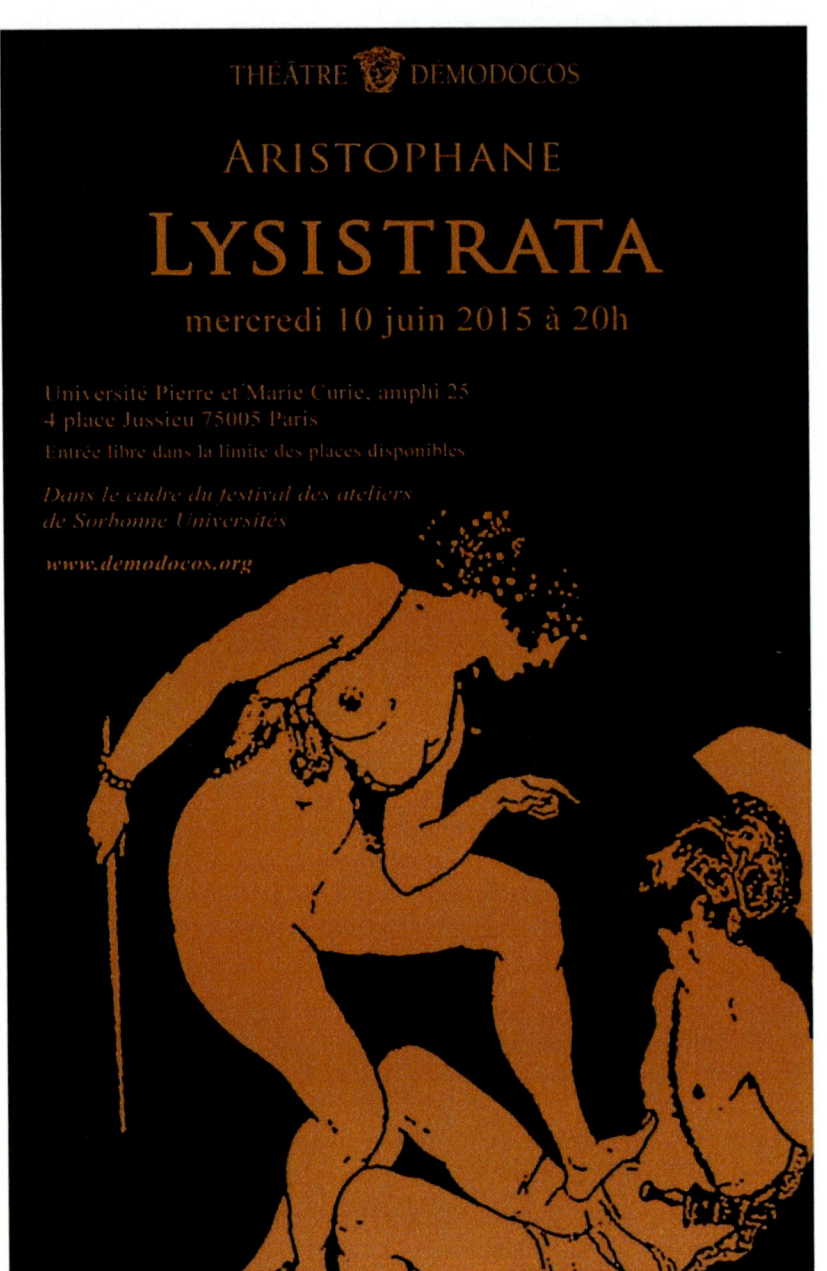

THÉÂTRE DEMODOCOS

ARISTOPHANE

LYSISTRATA

mercredi 10 juin 2015 à 20h

Université Pierre et Marie Curie, amphi 25
4 place Jussieu 75005 Paris
Entrée libre dans la limite des places disponibles

*Dans le cadre du festival des ateliers
de Sorbonne Universités*

www.demodocos.org

Lysistrata:
This Play illustrates the possibility of Women Leaders rising to embrace Tolerance, Goodwill, and Compassion to bring a era of peace to the world.

The Return of the Mother Principle and Breastfeeding Culture to the world.

A Woman of Islam

In the theater of Dionysius – the birthplace of Western drama -- in the year 411 BC sat the Ancient Greeks, happily munching their figs and pomegranates, and was played out before them the comedies of Aristophanes, sex comedies of outrageous and glorious wit like "Lysistrata."

Two women speak. Lysistrata: "There are a lot of things about us women that sadden me, considering men see us as rascals." Calonice agrees: "As indeed we are!" These lines spoken at the beginning of the play, set the scene for the action that follows. Calonice represents the women of city states of Sparta and Athens then engaged in the Peloponnesian War. Lysistrata is an extraordinary woman with a large sense of individual and social responsibility, who convened the women to give them a firm hand and direction. With support from Lampito, the Spartan, Lysistrata persuades the other women to withhold sexual privileges from their menfolk as a means of forcing them to end the interminable war. The women are reluctant but the deal is sealed with a solemn oath, in which the women abjure all their sexual pleasures, including a sexual position known as the Lioness on the Cheese Grater.

The play is peppered with such hilarious scenes as the struggle of Old Men and Old Women for control of the state treasury at the Acropolis without which the men cannot fund their war; a magistrate reflecting on the hysterical nature of women, their devotion to wine, promiscuous sex and exotic cults, blaming the men for poor supervision of their womenfolk, and demanding silver from the state treasury to buy oars for the fleet; groups of unruly women with such unruly names as "seed-market-porridge-vegetable-sellers" and "garlic-innkeeping-bread-sellers"; Lysistrata explaining frustrations women feel at a time of war when the men make stupid decisions that affect everyone, and their wives' opinions are not listened to, and saying that war will be a woman's business from now on, expressing the pity she feels for young, childless women, wasting their child-bearing years and ageing at home while the men are away on endless campaigns; the women desperate for sex beginning to desert on the silliest pretexts (for example, one woman says she has to go home to air her fabrics by spreading them on the bed); Kinesias, the husband of Myrrhine who teases him with sex on the spot, exasperating him with delays until finally denying him; a Spartan herald with an obvious erection, listening to the magistrate, also with an obvious erection.

As peace talks commence, Lysistrata introduces the Spartan and Athenian delegates to a gorgeous young woman called Reconciliation. The delegates cannot take their eyes off the young woman; and meanwhile, Lysistrata scolds both sides for past errors of judgment. The delegates briefly squabble over the peace terms; but, with Reconciliation before them and the burden of sexual deprivation still heavy upon them, they quickly overcome their differences and retire to the Acropolis for celebrations.

This story illustrates the grand possibility of women leaders rising in the world to curb the men's propensity for war and mayhem, perhaps expand the culture of Scientific Humanism to embrace Tolerance, Compassion and Goodwill, to promote a synthesis of all faiths as basis of peace for all time, a family-oriented, mother-directed multiplicity of deities in a common pantheon, perhaps for millenniums ahead, like the ancient civilizations. This is not to hard to aspire for, since the God of the three modern religions are one and the same – Yahweh, God the Father and Allah. Surely the cult of Mary can co-exist with the Cult of Fatima, Moses with Jesus and Mohammed.

In the 7th Century, Prophet Mohammad was considered a Feminist who

- Prohibited the practice of burying alive unwanted female babies
- Made education a woman's right
- Gave the women the right to inherit property
- Stated that sex satisfaction is a woman's right

In the 20th Century his Feminism became obsolete:

- Koran Law gives women ½ of the inheritance of men
- Women's testimony is worth ½ that of men
- Compensation for the death of the women is ½ that of men
- To prove rape, one must have the testimonies of 4 men testifying to actual penetration
- The legal age for girls is 9 years, for boys is 14 years

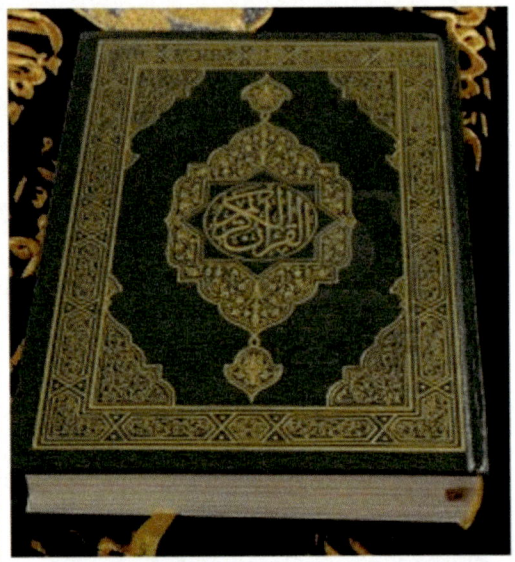

The women of Israel and Christianity are successfully overcoming the inferior status that Judaism and Christianity have long imposed on them. But it is different with the women of Islam. They are treated like chattel, like animals. It was not always so. We quote Time Magazine in full:

For his day, the Prophet Muhammad was a feminist. The doctrine he laid out as the revealed word of God considerably improved the status of women in 7th century Arabia. In local pagan society, it was the custom to bury alive unwanted female newborns; Islam prohibited the practice. Women had been treated as possessions of their husbands; Islamic law made the education of girls a sacred duty and gave women the right to own and inherit property. Muhammad even decreed that sexual satisfaction was a woman's entitlement. He was a liberal at home as well as in the pulpit. The Prophet darned his own garments and among his wives and concubines had a trader, a warrior, a leatherworker and an imam.

Of course, ancient advances do not mean that much to women 14 centuries later if reform is, rather than a process, a historical blip subject to reversal. While it is impossible, given their diversity, to paint one picture of women living under Islam today, it is clear that the religion has been used in most Muslim countries not to liberate but to entrench inequality. The Taliban, with its fanatical subjugation of the female sex, occupies an extreme, but it nevertheless belongs on a continuum that includes, not so far down the line, Saudi Arabia, Kuwait, Pakistan and the relatively moderate states of Egypt and Jordan. Where Muslims have afforded women the greatest degree of equality -- in Turkey -- they have done so by overthrowing Islamic precepts in favor of secular rule. As Riffat Hassan, professor of religious studies at the University of Louisville, puts it, "The way Islam has been practiced in most Muslim societies for centuries has left millions of Muslim women with battered bodies, minds and souls."

Part of the problem dates to Muhammad. Even as he proclaimed new rights for women, he enshrined their inequality in immutable law, passed down as God's commandments and eventually recorded in scripture. The Koran allots daughters half the inheritance of sons. It decrees that a woman's testimony in court, at least in financial matters, is worth half that of a man's. Under Shari'a, or Muslim law, compensation for the murder of a woman is half the going rate for men. In many Muslim countries, these directives are incorporated into contemporary law. For a woman to prove rape in Pakistan, for example, four adult males of "impeccable" character must witness the penetration, in accordance with Shari'a.

Family law in Islamic countries generally follows the prescriptions of scripture. This is so even in a country like Egypt, where much of the legal code has been secularized. In Islam, women can have only one spouse, while men are permitted four. The legal age for girls to marry tends to be very young. Muhammad's favorite wife, A'isha, according to her biographer, was six when they wed, nine when the marriage was consummated. In Iran the legal age for marriage is nine for girls, 14 for boys. The law has occasionally been exploited by pedophiles, who marry poor young girls from the provinces, use and then abandon them. In 2000 the Iranian Parliament voted to raise the minimum age for girls to 14, but this year, a legislative oversight body dominated by traditional clerics vetoed the move. An attempt by conservatives to abolish Yemen's legal minimum age of 15 for girls failed, but local experts say it is rarely enforced anyway. (The onset of puberty is considered an appropriate time for a marriage to be consummated.)

A Pakistani, she was shot in the head at 15, fought for her life and girls' education. She now lives in England.

IMPACT

Malala Yousafzai, Shot By Taliban For Supporting Girls' Education, Celebrates Straight-As

The youngest-ever winner of the Nobel Peace Prize has turned down hundreds of interviews to focus on schoolwork.

🕐 08/21/2015 11:00 am ET | Updated Aug 24, 2015

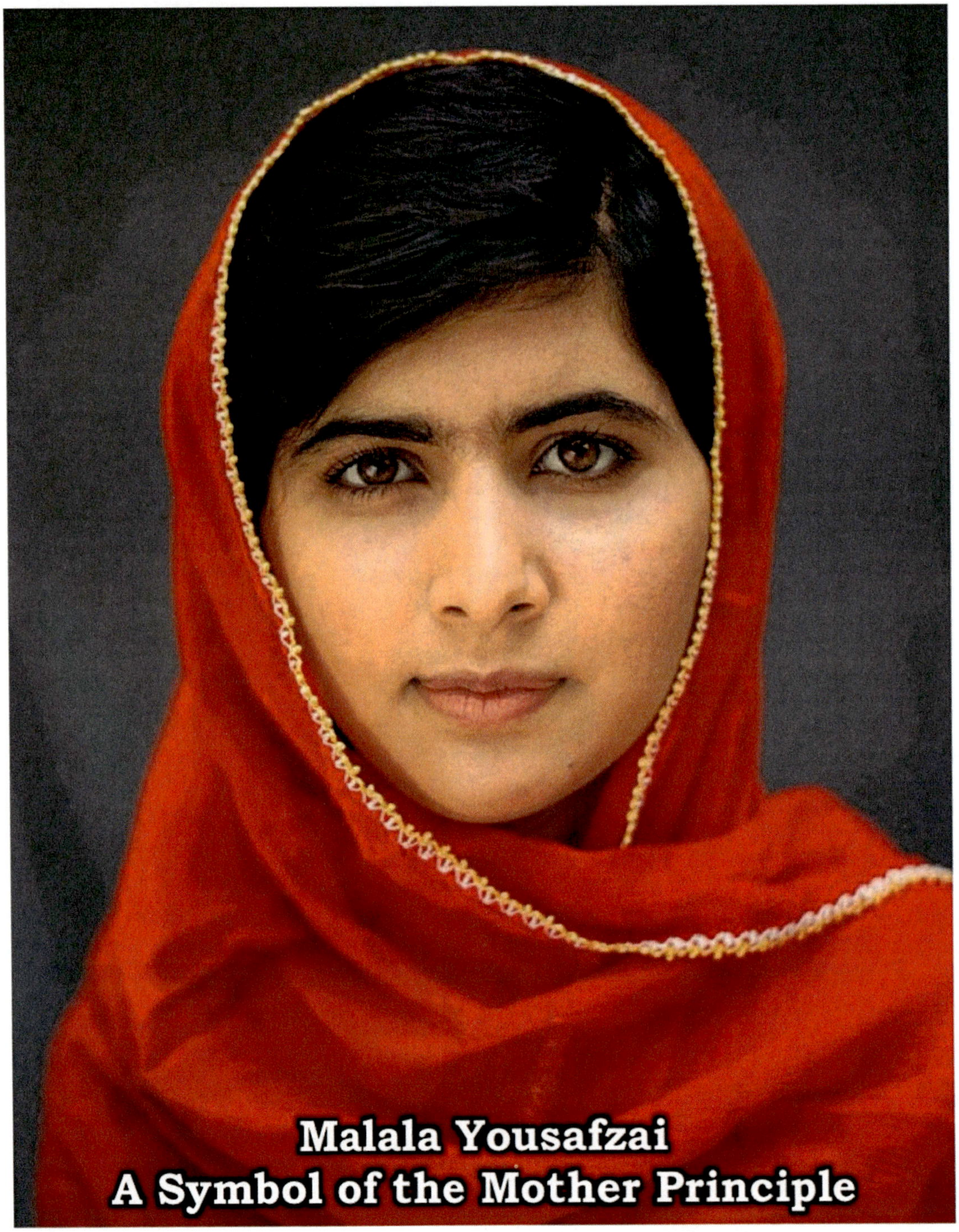

Malala Yousafzai
A Symbol of the Mother Principle

Wives in Islamic societies face great difficulty in suing for divorce, but husbands can be released from their vows virtually on demand, in some places merely by saying "I divorce you" three times. Though in most Muslim states, divorces are entitled to alimony, in Pakistan it lasts only three months, long enough to ensure the woman isn't pregnant. The same three-month rule applies even to the Muslim minority in India. There, a national law provides for long-term alimony, but to appease Islamic conservatives, authorities exempted Muslims.

Fear of poverty keeps many Muslim women locked in bad marriages, as does the prospect of losing their children. Typically, fathers win custody of boys over the age of six and girls after the onset of puberty. Maryam, an Iranian woman, says she has stayed married for 20 years to a philandering opium addict she does not love because she fears losing guardianship of her teenage daughter. "Islam supposedly gives me the right to divorce," she says. "But what about my rights afterward?" Women's rights are compromised further by a section in the Koran, sura 4:34, that has been interpreted to say that men have "pre-eminence" over women or that they are "overseers" of women. The verse goes on to say that the husband of an insubordinate wife should first admonish her, then leave her to sleep alone and finally beat her. Wife beating is so prevalent in the Muslim world that social workers who assist battered women in Egypt, for example, spend much of their time trying to convince victims that their husbands' violent acts are unacceptable.

This is the saga of Malala Yousafzai. Malala started to speak out for girl's rights at the age of 11, when the Taliban banned girls from going to school in the Swat Valley in Pakistan. Malala defied the rules and kept on going to school. Her life was under threat and at times she had to go into hiding. On 9 October 2012, when she was 15, on her way home from school, a man dressed in white with face hidden behind a bandana, boarded the bus she was riding, and asked, "Which one of you is Malala?" None of the girls in the back of the minibus said a word. But their faces revealed who Malala is. The man raised his pistol and fired three rapid shots. The first bullet hit Malala in the head. But Malala survived. The Taliban thought they could silence Malala by killing her. Instead they gave her an even stronger voice, which can now be heard all over the world. Malala is determined to continue her struggle for every child's right to an education. She believes that education is the future, and that one child, one teacher, one book and one pen can change the world. Under her care is the Malala Fund, created to fund the education of Muslim girls. All over the world, great foundations are funding the fight against sex trafficking, prostitution, domestic violence against women, and also the fight against opposition to Reproductive Health, equal pay for women, breastfeeding as the norm for the nurture of the human race.

The saga of Malala is an inspiration to the women of the Muslim world, and will no doubt, in the course of time, bring about the liberation of all women of Islam, in conjunction with the rise of Woman Leaders and the nannies, nurses and caregivers of the Philippines to frustrate the Talibans, the Al Qaeda and the ISIS of this world. Good will always prevail over evil. Truth will always prevail over Untruth. Beauty will always prevail over Ugliness. All in the fullness of time. And when all the stories have been told, and all the songs have been sung, and all there is to be has become, civilization will flower again under the family-oriented, mother-directed synthesis of all religions based on tolerance, goodwill and compassion --- to last for millenniums in the future. And we Filipinos, with all our faults and idiosyncrasies, hope to be the First Citizens of that world.

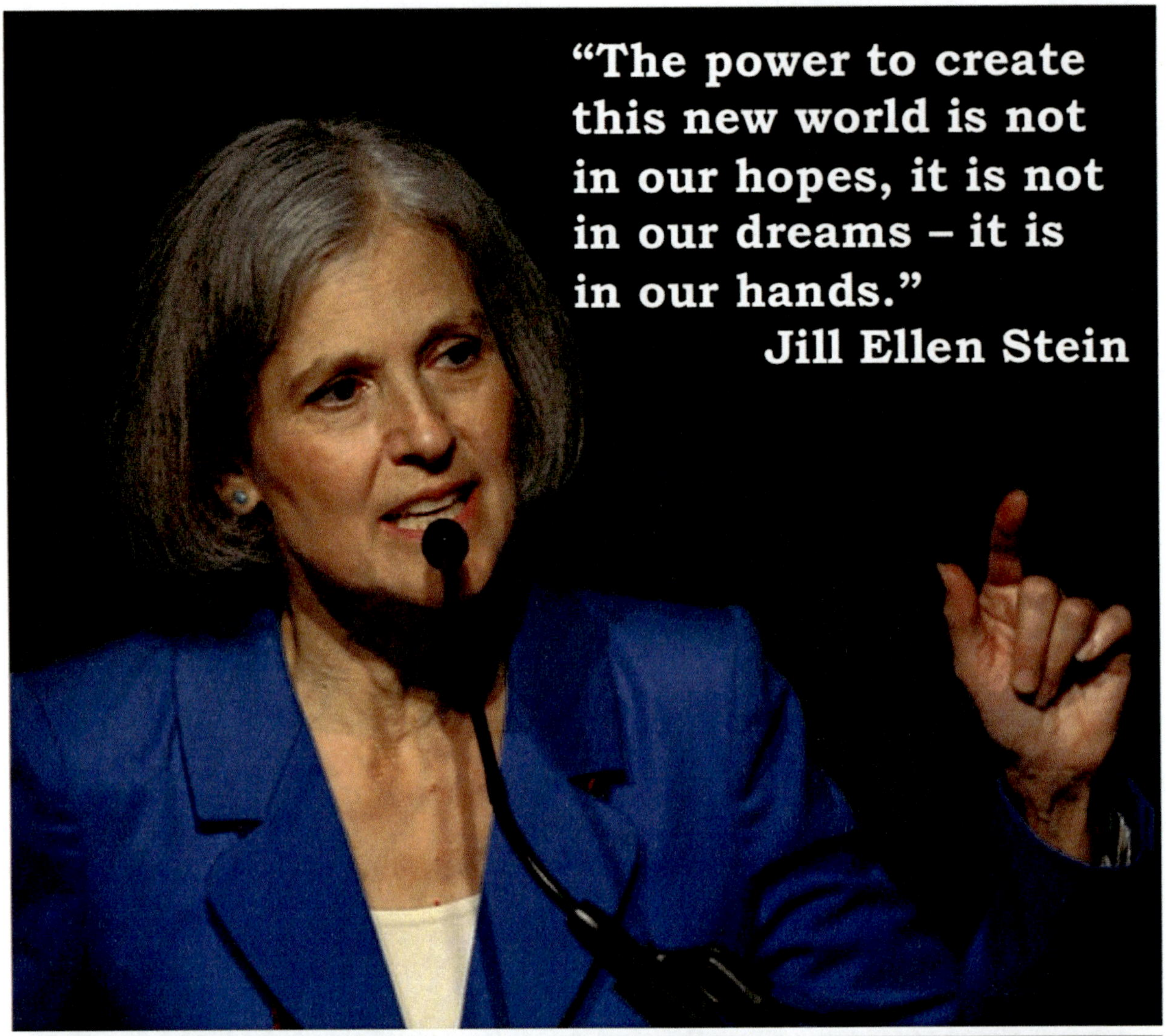

"The power to create this new world is not in our hopes, it is not in our dreams – it is in our hands."
Jill Ellen Stein

Stein, a Jew, is the candidate of the Green Party for the Presidency of the United States, in the year 2016

A Symbol of the Mother Principle

A Woman of the Jewish Race

Surely there must somebody in our cock-eyed world with a plan to save the world from itself, to save human beings from themselves – a complete comprehensive plan, well-thought out, a clear and coherent plan that covers all the problems that beset this planet. We seek and we found a woman of the Jewish race, Jill Stein, a candidate of the Green Party for the Presidency of the United States, the most powerful country on earth. We print here, courtesy of Wikipedia, the entire story of her life, because to us, here is the Messiah that the Jews had long yearned for, not to save the Jewish faith, but to save the entire human race.

Jill Ellen Stein (born May 14, 1950) is an American physician, activist, and politician. Stein was the presidential nominee of the Green Party in 2012, in which she received 469,501 votes (0.4%). She has also twice been a candidate for Governor of Massachusetts—in 2002 and 2010. She is currently the Green Party's nominee for President of the United States in the 2016 election, with a platform of Power to the People stated thus:

"My Power to the People Plan creates deep system change, moving from the greed and exploitation of corporate capitalism to a human-centered economy that puts people, planet and peace over profit. It offers direct answers to the economic, social, and ecological crises brought on by both corporate political parties. And it empowers the American people to fix our broken political system and make real the promise of democracy. This plan will end unemployment and poverty; avert climate catastrophe; build a sustainable, just economy; and recognize the dignity and human rights of everyone in our society and our world. The power to create this new world is not in our hopes, it's not in our dreams - it's in our hands."

Jill Stein was born in Chicago, the daughter of Gladys (née Wool) and Joseph Stein, and was raised in Highland Park, Illinois. She is Jewish, and her family attended Chicago's North Shore Congregation Israel, a Reform synagogue. Her parents were both from Russian Jewish families and Stein was raised in a Reform Jewish household although she now considers herself agnostic. Stein is married to Richard Rohrer, who is also a physician. They live in Lexington, Massachusetts, and have two adult sons.

In 1973, Stein graduated *magna cum laude* from Harvard University, where she studied psychology, sociology, and anthropology. She then attended Harvard Medical School and graduated in 1979. After graduating from Harvard Medical School, Stein practiced internal medicine for 25 years. Stein practiced medicine at Beth Israel Deaconess Medical Center, Simmons College Health Center, and Harvard Pilgrim Health Care, and also served as an instructor of medicine at Harvard Medical School. Stein retired from practicing and teaching medicine in 2005 and 2006, respectively.

In 2008, she helped formulate a successful "Secure Green Future" ballot initiative that called upon legislators to accelerate efforts to move the Massachusetts economy to renewable energy and make development of green jobs a priority. Other organizations Stein has worked with include Clean Water Action, Toxic Action Center, Global Climate Convergence, Physicians for a National Health Program, and Massachusetts Medical Society. She received the "Not in Anyone's Backyard Award" in 1998 and the "Children's Health Hero Award" in 2000 from Clean Water Action, and the "Citizen Award" from Toxic Action Center in 1999 and the "Friend of the Earth Award" from Salem State College in 2004.

Jill Ellen Stein

- A doctor of medicine
- An environmentalist
- A singer and composer
- An advocate of:
    ➤ campaign finance reform
    ➤ employment as a right
    ➤ health care as a right
    ➤ racial justice
    ➤ human rights
and we hope of breastfeeding as the norm for the nurture of the future citizens of the world.

As a medical doctor and researcher, Stein has published several materials and teaching plans, and has testified before legislative panels as well as local and state governmental bodies. In 2000, she co-authored the scientific report *In Harm's Way: Toxic Threats to Child Development*, and in 2009 co-authored the report *Environmental Threats to Healthy Aging*. These reports have been widely cited and translated into numerous languages. She has also co-authored articles about health in publications such as The Huffington Post. In 2009, Stein developed a teaching plan called "Healthy People, Healthy Planet" that was supported by Boston University and has been presented at other schools and universities.

Stein is also an advocate for campaign finance reform. In 1998, she helped campaign for the Clean Elections Law in Massachusetts. The law was later repealed by a Democratic majority legislature, leading Stein to leave the Democratic party for good and join the Green Party. Stein was one of several activists involved with the Clean Elections Law to file a complaint in the Supreme Judicial Court for Suffolk County in 2002 against William F. Galvin, the Secretary of the Commonwealth of Massachusetts, over the state's failure to successfully implement the law. Stein has also served on the board of *Mass Voters for Fair Elections* and has campaigned for implementing instant runoff voting in Massachusetts.

Alongside her political career, Jill Stein also developed multiple musical albums with collaborator Ken Selcer in the folk-rock band Somebody's Sister. Jill is able to play the conga and djembe drums and guitar. During the 1990s and 2000s, the duo released four studio albums: *Flashpoint*, *Somebody's Sister*, *Green Sky*, and *Circuits To The Sun*. Many of the songs focus on issues similar to those Stein emphasizes in her political career: peace, justice, and climate action. The pair also often performed at live events, such as the 2008 Green-Rainbow Convention in Leominster, Massachusetts. The band was twice named semi-finalists in Musician's contest of best unsigned bands in 1996 and 1998.

Key points of the Power to the People Plan, presented by Jill Stein as Presidential Candidate, to the American people:
- **A Green New Deal:** Create millions of jobs by transitioning to 100% clean renewable energy by 2030, and investing in public transit, sustainable agriculture, and conservation.
- **Jobs as a Right:** Create living-wage jobs for every American who needs work, replacing unemployment offices with employment offices. Advance workers' rights to form unions, achieve workplace democracy, and keep a fair share of the wealth they create.
- **End Poverty:** Guarantee economic human rights, including access to food, water, housing, and utilities, with effective anti-poverty programs to ensure every American a life of dignity.
- **Health Care as a Right:** Establish an improved "Medicare For All" single-payer public health insurance program to provide everyone with quality health care, at huge savings.
- **Education as a Right:** Abolish student debt to free a generation of Americans from debt servitude. Guarantee tuition-free, world-class public education from pre-school through university. End high stakes testing and public school privatization.
- **A Just Economy:** Set a $15/hour federal minimum wage. Break up "too-big-to-fail" banks and democratize the Federal Reserve. Reject gentrification as a model of economic development. Support development of worker and community cooperatives and small businesses. Make Wall Street, big corporations, and the rich pay their fair share of taxes. Create democratically run public banks and utilities. Replace corporate trade agreements with fair trade agreements.

Israeli Prime Minister Benjamin Netanhahu

Jewish Jill Ellen Stein is a loud critic of Israel and its prime minister, accusing it of apartheid, assassinations, blockades, violation of treaties forbidding nuclear proliferation, indefinite detention, collective punishment, and defiance of International Law – and supports Boycott, Divestment and Sanctions against Israel, as well as Saudi Arabia and other nations, friend or foe.

- **Protect Mother Earth:** Lead on a global treaty to halt climate change. End destructive energy extraction: fracking, tar sands, offshore drilling, oil trains, mountaintop removal, and uranium mines. Protect our public lands, water supplies, biological diversity, parks, and pollinators. Label GMOs, and put a moratorium on GMOs and pesticides until they are proven safe. Protect the rights of future generations.
- **Racial Justice Now:** End police brutality and mass incarceration. Create a Truth and Reconciliation Commission to understand and eliminate the legacy of slavery that lives on as pervasive racism in the economy, education, housing and health. Ensure that communities control their police rather than police controlling our communities, by establishing police review boards and full time investigators to look in to all cases of death in police custody. Demilitarize the police.
- **Freedom and Equality:** Expand women's rights, protect LGBTQIA+ people from discrimination, defend indigenous rights and lands, and create a welcoming path to citizenship for immigrants. Protect the free Internet, legalize marijuana/hemp, and treat substance abuse as a public health problem, not a criminal problem.
- **Justice for All:** Restore our Constitutional rights, terminate unconstitutional surveillance and unwarranted spying, end persecution of government and media whistleblowers, close Guantanamo, abolish secret kill lists, and repeal indefinite detention without charge or trial.
- **Peace and Human Rights:** Establish a foreign policy based on diplomacy, international law, and human rights. End the wars and drone attacks, cut military spending by at least 50% and close the 700+ foreign military bases that are turning our republic into a bankrupt empire. Stop U.S. support and arms sales to human rights abusers, and lead on global nuclear disarmament.
- **Empower the People:** Abolish corporate personhood. Protect voters' rights by establishing a constitutional right to vote. Enact electoral reforms that break the big money stranglehold and create truly representative democracy: public campaign financing, ranked-choice voting, proportional representation, and open debates.

For more than half a century, statesmen are trying to resolve the problem of the Jewish occupation of Arab lands, that helped launch Islam's holy war against the United States and Western civilization, given the intransigence of the Jewish lobby in the USA that insists on arming Israel with a nuclear arsenal, in violation of treaties forbidding nuclear proliferation, and making Israel the tail that wags the American dog. Jill Stein has been highly critical of Israel, accusing the Israeli government of "apartheid, assassination, illegal settlements, blockades, building of nuclear bombs, indefinite detention, collective punishment, and defiance of international law." She regards Israeli Prime Minister Benjamin Netanyahu as a war criminal, and supports the Boycott, Divestment and Sanctions campaign against Israel, even as she supports the same kind of treatment against Saudi Arabia and other nations, friend or foe, that violates human rights. The fact that Jill Stein is of the Jewish race, a potential president of the powerful United States, and a woman, makes her all the more the harbinger of things to come – a symbol of the Mother Principle that will rule the future.

Summing Up

- First century Jews thrown out of the Roman Empire for being disruptive and subversive.
- Jews migrated to Europe, specially to Germany where they were welcomed.
- The British Foreign Secretary promulgated the Balfour Declaration promising a homeland for the Jews in Palestine, an empty promise that undermined Jewish loyalty to Germany in World War I.
- Hitler blamed the Jews for Germany's defeat in World War I, unified Germany and led it it to World War II, and the Final Solution, the mass genocide of 6 million Jews.
- After World War II, the Jews are given a home in Palestine by the United Nations against the protestations of the Arab nations, giving birth to Radical Islam that is now heading a Jihad against the West that may lead to World War III.

Arthur James Balfour

United Nations Logo

The Summing Up

It is not impossible, the Transformation and the Transfiguration of the human race. In my lifetime, I have witnessed the change that came about to Imperial Japan and Nazi Germany, the two most vicious, most tyrannical regimes during the World War II, in the hands of Supreme Commander General Douglas MacArthur, and under the aegis of the Marshall Plan devised by US Secretary of War George Marshall, respectively, into peaceful, responsible and compassionate nations.

To sum up my thesis, I have taken my readers through a journey of the mind through millenniums of four major ancient civilizations (Egypt, Greece, Rome and China) whose common characteristic is that they existed under religions that were family-oriented and mother-directed, where a multiplicity of gods occupied a common pantheon without bigotry or discrimination and based on tolerance, goodwill and compassion. These four great civilizations came to end with the rise of three alpha-male father-directed religions (Judaism, Christianity and Islam) with one common God and an uncommon rivalry and murderous antagonism toward each other, and among the sects within each other. Ancient civilizations worship different gods and tolerated each other. Modern religions worship the same God (Yahweh, God the Father, and Allah) and cannot stand each other.

It started in the first century AD when the Jews were ejected from their home in Palestine and from the Roman Empire. It continued when the Holy Roman Empire of the Catholic Church replaced Ancient Rome. Interminable wars and religious persecution culminated in first World War, World War I, that ended with the defeat of Germany. Germany relied on the loyalty of German Jews whom they graciously welcomed in their country. Then the Foreign Secretary of Great Britain with whom Germany was locked in mortal combat, issued the famous Balfour Declaration that promised the Jews a new national home in Palestine, an empty promise that appealed to all Zionist Jews all over the world including those in Germany. When Germany was defeated, the Germans felt betrayed by their Jews, and hated them for it.

Adolf Hitler exploited his people's hatred of the Jews to unite and re-arm the Germans and led them to the second World War, World War II during which Hitler devised the Nazi Final Solution, the Holocaust that sent 6 million Jews to the ovens of Buchenwald and Dachau. Instead of punishing the Nazis, the United Nations punished the Arabs by forcing them to suffer the return of the Jews to Palestine after 2,000 years of Diaspora. So the Arabic nations of Islam, radicalized by this intrusion are engaged in a holy war that Pope Francis describes as the beginning of World War III. World War I was fought only in Europe. World War II was fought in Europe and Asia. World War III is being fought in every city and in every nation with acts of terrorism, and threatens eventually to involve the whole planet in a nuclear war, with the Jews in the middle of it.

We explored the possibility that women leaders long considered inferior by the men, will rise to promote tolerance, goodwill and compassion among religions. I do not really expect a return to the old religions of the ancient world, nor do I advocate the demise of the new religions of the modern world. I do believe in One God and I do believe that Science will eventually confirm God's existence.

Summing Up

- In Ancient Civilizations, there was a COMMON PANTHEON of DIFFERENT GODS – and no religious persecution.
- In Modern Civizations, there is a COMMON GOD worshipped by all – but religious persecution, notions of racial superiority, and institutionalized genocide exist.
- In the Future, we hope the Mother Principle will be reestablished where Faith, Hope and Charity which are divisive, are replaced by Tolerance, Goodwill and Compassion.
- Thus will every man be welcomed into any synagogue, church or mosque, to worship the God common to all.

The Trinity of Ancient Egypt

Pope Francis greets Ecumenical Patriarch Bartholomew.

God the Father of Modern Christianity

Prior to the 20th century, most scientists believed that our universe never had a beginning, that mass, space, time and energy had always existed. Then in 1928 Edwin Hubble discovered that the universe is expanding, and using its velocity and direction, he calculated that the universe was born 13.8 billion years ago, from one explosion called the Big Bang, at a single time from a single pinpoint, from nothing, just like it says in the Bible, Genesis 1:1. The scientists have struggled so long up the mountain of knowledge, only to find that Bible scholars were already there at the top long before they arrived. If the rate of expansion of the Big Bang were a fraction less, the universe would have re-collapsed even before it reached its present size; if it were a fraction more, stars and galaxies could not have been formed, and we wouldn't be here. Conditions for life to exist (the existence and distribution of elements; the size, temperature, relative proximity of stars and planets) need to be just right that the chance against it to happen from a chance explosion of the Big Bang, defies the laws of probability – calculated to be one chance against a trillion repeated 12 times, or 10^{144}, or 1 followed by 144 zeroes -- equivalent to the chance of a blind person finding one specific grain of sand from all the beaches in the world, or one person winning a mega-dollar lotto, a thousand consecutive times, with the same set of numbers. The only logical conclusion is that life came into being by deliberate design of a Superior Intellect, like the Bible says. Then in 1953 Watson and Crick discovered the DNA in every cell of every living thing, a mere pinhead of which contains information equivalent to a stack of paperback books that would encircle the earth 5,000 times – an extremely complex software that reveals such intelligence that it staggers the imagination. There must be a God, a Supreme Being with the Intelligence to create our Universe.

I do believe in God, and the secularization of religions that will eliminate the murderous rivalry that results in religious persecution. Already in the world of white Europeans, great cathedrals are being emptied of white worshippers and filled with tourists. And in small chapels by the side of the great altars, gather every Sunday, people of my blood, Filipinos, who have lost their sense of nationalism and embraced the world as its First Citizens. And women dominate our Filipino society. American women won the vote 144 years after the US Declaration of Independence; Filipino women won the vote only 32 years after the Philippine Declaration of Independence. Filipinos elected two women presidents long before the Americans elected even one. Filipinos had women senators and women Supreme Court Justices long before Americans had some. Filipinos now have a woman Chief Justice while the Americans take their sweet time having one. For women in politics, the Philippines has shown the way for the rest of the world.

I do believe in God, and I believe in the cult of Mary that promises the resurgence of the Mother Principle that promotes tolerance, goodwill and compassion. I believe that man is at his best in the moment he bows his head to his God. And I look forward to the day when every worshiper is welcomed into any synagogue, any church and any mosque everywhere to pay homage to the One God we all share.

I do believe that someday we will eventually expunge the notions of racial superiority and institutionalized genocide that has infected the white races of the Christian Era, the excesses of Colonialism and Capitalism that exploited the colored races and the workers of the world, the sectarian violence that has characterized the rivalry of Orange Protestants and Green Catholics in Ireland, the rivalry between Hindus and Muslims in India, the Sikhs and the Tamils in Shri-Lanka, the Christians and the Muslims in the Philippines, the Shiites and the Sunnis among the Muslims, and Radical Islam against the world. Lasting peace will come only upon the resurgence of the Mother Principle among the all religions of the world.

Summing Up

The Mother Principle will be reestablished with

- The rise of Women Leaders and Unconditional Love women are capable of, along with Breastfeeding as the Norm for the nourishment of the future citizens of the world.
- The loss of divisive Nationalism, and the Diaspora of the First Citizens of the World, whose nannies in the home of the rich rock the cradles that will rule the world.
- The World Olympics conducted every four years as it was in Ancient Greece, with a year-long Mandatory Truce on all wars, as mandated by a new Geneva Conference on the conduct of war.

Hands that rock the cradle rule the world

Simone Biles
Olympian Gymnast

Mother Teresa
Symbol of the Mother Principle

Dara Torres
Olympian Swimmer

In olden golden days, the Greeks would suspend the wars they were waging, to engage in peaceful athletic competitions in the Olympics at the foot of Mount Olympus. In modern days, we suspended the Olympics that was scheduled in 1916 and in 1940, because we were engaged in fighting World War I and World War II respectively. I would like to see the day when wars will voluntarily be suspended under mandatory truce, every four years, as in ancient times, for one full year to allow our athletes to train and compete freely and peacefully in the both the Summer and Winter Olympics. Such mandatory truce should be included among the terms of the Geneva Convention governing the rules of engagement in war. That should give our peoples time to ponder on the awful consequences of continuing the pursuit of war, and our diplomats time to negotiate further terms peacefully to end the hostilities of war.

I am sorry to have to say this, but the most Godly virtues are not Faith, Hope, Love and Charity, but Tolerance, Goodwill and Compassion. Faith, Hope, Love and Charity are generated internally in ourselves, while Tolerance, Goodwill and Compassion are extended outwardly toward the embrace of others. Faith, based on a body of beliefs, is what separates one religion from another, and is basically divisive. Hope is based on great expectations for one's self primarily, and not necessarily for others; for others it is not Hope, but Goodwill. Love is something that must be given voluntarily, and has to be earned by the recipient; it cannot be obligatory or mandatory. There is something about Charity that is disturbingly patronizing, specially from the rich to the poor, *id est*, patronizing for the rich, and somewhat debasing for the poor. From the rich to the rich is not Charity, neither is there Charity between the poor and the poor; it is merely Sharing what one has. From the rich to the poor, from the rich to the rich, from the poor to the poor, the Giving is always voluntary; mandatory giving is nothing but extortion.

It is not really necessary to have Faith, Hope, Love or Charity in order for peace and consensus to prevail. But it is important to have Tolerance, Goodwill and Compassion in order to have peaceful coexistence, based on consensus and mutual respect. Tolerance, Goodwill and Compassion can be made obligatory and mandatory, as they are so implied in our basic tenets of Freedom of Thought, Freedom of Religion, Freedom from Hunger, Freedom from Poverty, Freedom of the Press, Freedom of Information, and Academic Freedom, and embodied in the statement, "I may disagree with what you believe or say, but I will defend to the death your right to believe and say it." To be truly free, we must be truly tolerant, compassionate and full of goodwill.

So it is really important that we enshrine in all our religions, specially into Judaism, Christianity and Islam, the truly Godly virtues of Tolerance, Goodwill and Compassion. So it is really important to elevate our respect and regard for Women to a level equal to, if not above those we have for Men, because women have inherent qualities for nurturing and unconditional love, free from excessive sex obsession and bigotry, so necessary to create a regimen of Tolerance, Goodwill and Compassion in our Society. We respect the Women of CNN, and take exception to Women embedded in the political section of Fox News, who are generally regarded as spiteful, opinionated, intolerant, and full of ill-will, with shrill voices carefully calibrated in a nagging mode to a maximum degree, sounding like fingernails scratching on the blackboard, or like cats on hot tin roof.

So it is really important to have the Mother Principle reestablished in the world, so that we are all free and welcomed in peace into any synagogue, church or mosque as brothers and sisters, under the fatherhood of ONE we all worship, coming to us with many names: Yahweh, God and Allah.

Summing Up

- The Roman Catholic will eventually open its doors to married priests and priestesses
- The Mother Principle will be served by resolving the 150-year battle of the Milk Companies and the US Government against Breastfeeding as the Norm for the nourishment of the future citizens of the world.
- Breastfeeding is the most wide-spread and cheapest strategy for the alleviation of poverty.
- Breastfeeding provides the Social Capital for the Life-long Health, Emotional Stability and Intellectual Development of the future citizens of the world.

Pope Francis and Archbishop Antje Jackelén of a Protestant Church in Sweden discuss one of the glaring differences between their churches: the role of women..

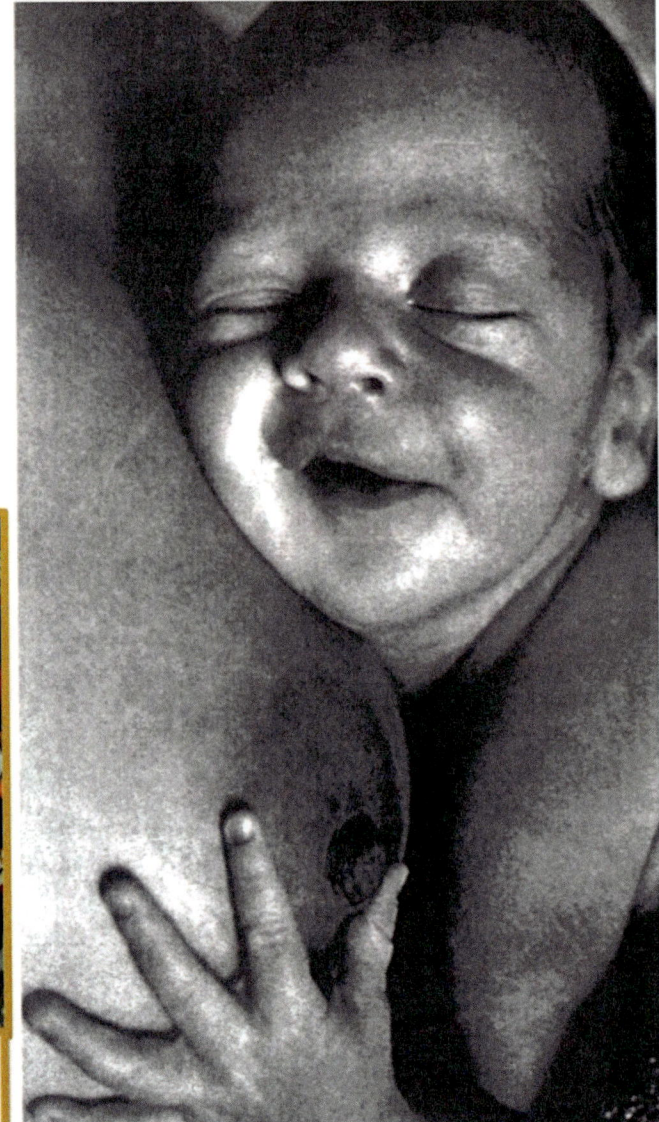

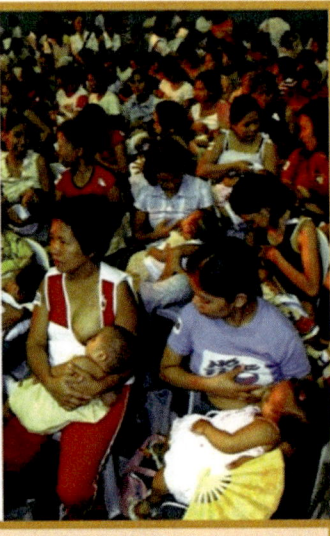

Philippines' Guinness World Record on Simultaneous Breastfeeding

How will the return of the Mother Principle affect the Holy Roman Catholic Church, the largest religious organization of all time, of 1.2 billion parishioners, the longest lasting, existing for two thousand years, the most male-dominated, led by a long unbroken line of 266 Popes from St. Peter the Apostle to the present Pope Francis I, the most wide-spread, the most influential, the most conservative in the entire world?? It may be surmised that the longevity of the church may be attributed to its vows of chastity that avoids the inbreeding and corruption that have been the bane and extinction of family dynasties. The downside is that many of Catholic priests have been found to be homosexuals who were molesters of the children under their care. In a Catholic country like the Philippines, in one particular province 70% of the secular priests have families and are living in sin. Many priests and bishops are corrupt accepting favors from government and corporate draculas, living it up with wine, women, and song while Catholic nuns pray silently and do the pious duties of the church.

There is absolutely nothing in the basic tenets of the Catholic Church that forbid priests from having families, or forbid women from achieving priesthood. Pope Francis says no women priests is forever, but he won't live that long. It is entirely possible for the Church of the future to admit priestesses. The Eastern Rite of the Catholics Church allow the ordination of married priests. It is entirely possible in the future for priests to be allowed to marry, like Protestant ministers. We predict that sooner than later that women will take over the Church, that marriages may be allowed among priests and nuns, although the Pope (male or female) will probably remain single.

In our future world the Mother Principle must be served by resolving the 150 year old Milk Wars that Nestle , the Milk Companies and the US government have been waging against the mothers of the world, causing, according to the World Health Organization (WHO), 800,000 babies dying of improper feeding every year. The WHO condemned the unethical marketing policies and practices of these corporate draculas, and the UN passed several resolutions at the World Assembly on (1) International Code on the Marketing of Breastmilk Substitutes; (2) Global Strategy on Infant and Young Child Feeding; (3) Convention on the Rights of the Child; among many resolutions at the WHO, always against the vote of the USA. We hope to win this war, yes, we shall even train lactating nuns to nourish orphans.

As I write my last words, I turn pensive and my thoughts burn like candles and trail into smoke and are lost in shadows. I am already 92 years old and will die in a few years, so why am writing all these for? At this moment saunters into view another old man of 72 years of age, plagued by diabetes and clogged arteries, who will probably die before I do. He is a friend, a Filipino of Spanish blood, who inherited his money and spends his time taking siestas and doing good for his fellowmen, a veritable do-gooder and bleeding heart. He was introduced to me by a cousin, an old man of 77 years, a Filipino of German blood, whom we call Der Fuehrer because of his tendency to line up against the wall anyone who disagrees with him, and whom we tolerate because he pays for the food we eat when we are together. We three old men are known as the Unholy Trinity of Unmitigated Shit because we all talk dirty like our Philippine President "DoDirty" Duterte who calls Obama a son of a whore and the US Ambassador a frigging faggot.

Come in, I said to my Spanish friend, sit down and talk to me, talk dirty. "I have this tribe," he began, "who shit all the time and then move farther on after their shit infect the place they live in and cause diseases to fester."
"Don't knock shit," I answer, "It is the greatest factor in the development of the human race.

Summing Up

The role of shit in human development

- First Humans polluted their environment, dying of disease, moved on to other lands, eventually populating the earth.
- First humans ate mushrooms growing out of animal shit, containing hallucinatory drugs, making them dream dreams that blow their minds, of dark pasts and shining futures, and poetic fancies that enlarged their brains.

Stone Age man ate mushrooms: Oldest evidence for fungi in the human diet discovered in 19,000-year-old tooth plaque

- Anthropologists studied the teeth of a prehistoric woman nicknamed the Red Lady who was found in the El Mirón cave in eastern Cantabria, Spain
- The plaque showed signs of plant pollen and several mushroom spores
- It is the earliest evidence for humans eating mushrooms yet discovered
- Researchers say the mushrooms may have flavoured the Red Lady's diet

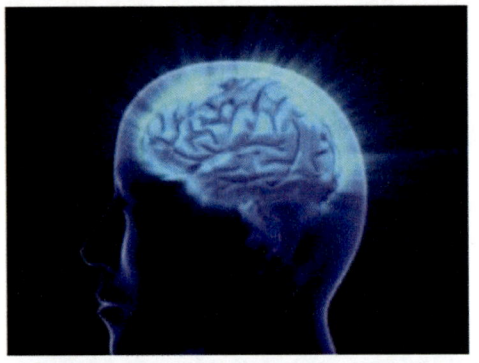

The Unholy Trinity of Unmitigated Shit

Larry Henares, 92

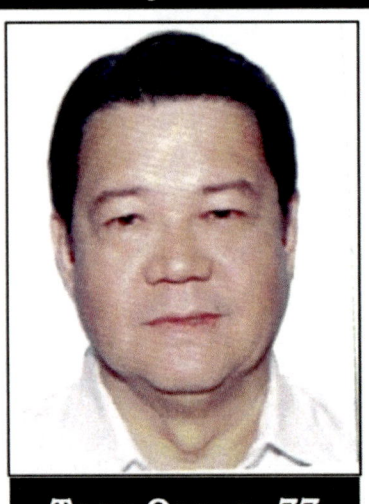

Tony Oppen, 77

Rod Alvarez, 72

The first humans populated the world by running away from their shit. To survive, they followed migratory animals who also shit all the time, and in their dung grow little mushrooms which our forefathers ate, 23 species of which cause hallucinatory dreams, making them dream of dreams that blow their minds, of dark pasts and shining futures, of insights and poetic fancies that expand their brains and their intelligence. Before you flush the toilet, take a good look at your shit, salute it and sing the national anthem. Shit made us human beings the superior animals that we are."

"As I was saying before you rudely interrupted me, this ancient tribe is made up of 2.8 million people occupying 2.2 million hectares of pure virgin forests, with a top soil one meter thick with rotten vegetation and human shit, incredibly fertile. The tribe is land rich and cash poor, their leader who is my adopted son is 36 years old and is only a high school graduate and worships Bathala," said my Spanish friend.

I answer, "My son has an opposite problem, he is a Harvard MBA graduate and he and his partner are cash rich and land poor. They manufacture abaca pulp which the Japanese use to make their paper currency and the Europeans to make tea bags and security paper, and they cannot buy enough abaca, from Bicol, from Leyte and Davao, and from far-off Ecuador, for goodness' sake. They manufacture cooking oil from palm oil which they cannot get enough because they have only 8,000 hectares of palm trees and need 30,000 hectares more. Say do you think your adopted son can supply the lands my son needs? We will make your tribe incredibly rich!"

And he answers, "What will sudden wealth do to a stone age tribe? They will only spend it on alcohol, women, guns and fast cars, and kill each other for money and power. What they really need are jobs, roads, schools, churches, health clinics and townships, and someone to civilize them. Can your son provide those?"

I answer, "Well, my son may provide jobs and roads but he knows nothing about schools, churches, health clinics and townships."

My Spanish friend answers, "in which case, forget it," and left.

That night I had a dream, and called my friend back, "I have a Christian evangelist minister with a penchant for building schools for free education, clinics for free medical and dental services, hostels for the stranded, capital for the poor entrepreneurs, buses and transit tickets for senior citizens, and a TV and radio stations he leases from my son, which he uses to spread goodwill in four continents via satellite, in North and South America, Asia and the Middle East. He has a lot of money because of his rich foreign constituents and his tax-free status. He will usher your ancient tribe to the 21st century, and under the aegis of Breastfeeding and the Mother Principle, and a regimen of Tolerance, Goodwill and Compassion!"

My Spanish friend lifts his eyes to God in the highest, and moves his lips to intone the Book of Joel, Chapter 2, verse 28: "And it shall come to pass afterward, that I will pour out my spirit upon all flesh; and your sons and daughters will prophesy, your old men shall dream dreams, your young men shall see visions.".

And like the rational ancient Greeks who consulted the Oracle at Delphi, an old woman chewing laurel leaves in a dark cave, I prayed, "Give me a sign, my Lord!"

Pacquiao pounds Vargas to win WBO welterweight title

(UPDATED) Manny Pacquiao wins the WBO welterweight title for the third time with a unanimous decision over Jessie Vargas in Las Vegas

Ryan Songalia
@ryansongalia
Published 1:06 PM, November 06, 2016
Updated 1:37 AM, November 07, 2016

THE HUFFINGTON POST
INFORM • INSPIRE • ENTERTAIN • EMPOWER

ENTERTAINMENT   WELLNESS   WHAT'S WORKING   VOICES   VIDEO   ALL SECTIONS

FEARLESS DREAMERS *Presented by* AMERICAN FAMILY INSURANCE

THE CURSE IS OVER! After 108-Year Drought, Chicago Cubs Defeat Cleveland Indians To Win 2016 World Series

The Cubs beat the Cleveland Indians 8-7 in their first World Series win since 1908.

11/03/2016 12:52 am ET | Updated Nov 07, 2016

The GUIDON

Sports

Ateneo Blue Eagles snap the DLSU Green Archers' unbeaten run, defeating them 83-71

BY KIRBY G. JALANDONI • PUBLISHED 05 November, 2016 AT 9:35 PM

Photo by John P. Oranga

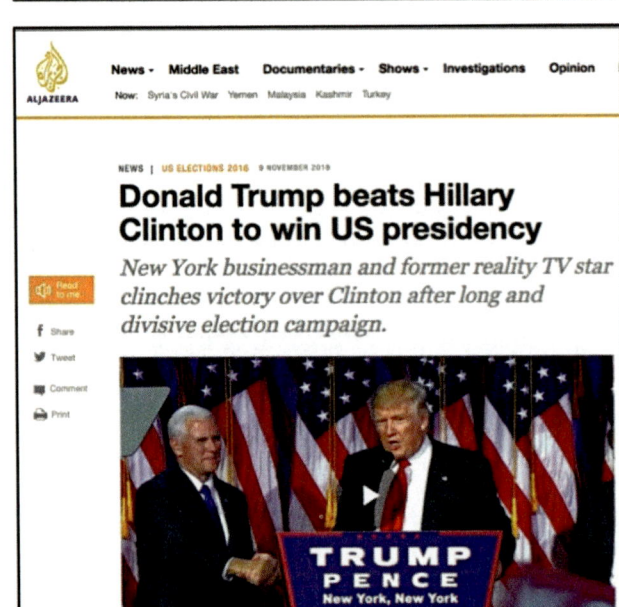

AL JAZEERA   News ·   Middle East   Documentaries ·   Shows ·   Investigations   Opinion
Now: Syria's Civil War   Yemen   Malaysia   Kashmir   Turkey

NEWS | US ELECTIONS 2016   9 NOVEMBER 2016

Donald Trump beats Hillary Clinton to win US presidency

New York businessman and former reality TV star clinches victory over Clinton after long and divisive election campaign.

My nurse, Julius Villapando, exclaimed, "Signs and portents? They are all around you on God's autumnal days, in the year of the Lord 2016. These are the Days of the Underdog. In the USA in baseball, the underdog Chicago Cubs beat the Cleveland Indians and emerged as champions after a drought of 108 years; in basketball, the underdog Los Angeles Lakers beat the champion Golden State Warriors. In the Philippines, in basketball the underdog University of the Philippines beat the mighty Ateneo; and the underdog Ateneo beat the champion La Salle. In boxing, underdog Manny Pacquiao took the welterweight crown of champion Jessie Vargas. In the US Presidential Elections, underdog Donald J. Trump wupped the bejesus out of Hillary R. Clinton. And, Mr. Henares, you have always been an underdog!"

That is right. I have always been an underdog. I have been a Rectonian nationalist underdog to the Little Brown Americans among my own people, I have been the Alexander Hamilton of my time vainly arguing for Industrialization against the World Bank and International Monetary Fund which decreed a pastoral economy for my country, I have been a breastfeeding advocate against the almighty Milk Companies. And if Donald Trump can upset the apple cart, so can I. Trump demolished the US Republican Party, and hijacked its presidential nomination; then he demolished the US Democratic Party and hijacked the Presidency of the United States. This obnoxious man with a foul mouth, bad manners and political incorrectness, turns out to be Horatio Hornblower, Baron Munchausen and Superman combined. The Americans deserve him.

Signs and Portents? These are not whispered prophesies of an old woman chewing laurel leaves in a dark cave, but thunderous clanging of church-bells at high noon in the public square!

The dreams of the old, the visions of the young, the prophesies of our sons and daughters. Let it be. Let it be. Let it be.

And so be it.

NOTE FROM THE AUTHOR:
This book is not original. It consists of various articles I wrote during my lifetime, plus quotes and paraphrases of many articles I have read that impressed me, including some from Sound and Light (*Son et Lumiere*) presentations, and illustrations from the Internet, of which I hope not to have violated any intellectual rights. I am already 92 years old and I write this book to enlighten, to inspire, to educate, to astound, to delight, to amuse, to imbue with a sense of wonder, those who will live after I die.

Larry Henares

Larry's late wife Cecilia, his inspiration

Larry Henares & Friends with President Syngman Rhee Father of South Korea 1955

Sukarno of Indonesia with Larry Henares 1961

Larry Henares

President Manuel Quezon

July 21, 1940

President Emilio Aguinaldo

ABOUT THE AUTHOR

Dr. Hilarion M. Henares, Jr., Doctor of Economics, will probably be known as the Alexander Hamilton of the Philippines. As Hamilton argued for his "Theory of Manufactures" to point the way to the United States' emergence as an industrial power, against Thomas Jefferson's advocacy of a "pastoral economy", so did Henares argue for Philippine Industrialization against American policy to keep the Philippines agricultural.

More than anyone else Henares is the most eloquent spokesman for the Philippine industrial middle class, and he articulated for his generation, the Nationalist Economic Philosophy for the advancement of the common masses. Said Education Secretary Juan Manuel, "Fiercely nationalistic, Henares chose as his field of battle the area of economics. There are many milestones that mark our way to economic emancipation and Henares was there first. He was a visionary, a gadfly, an achiever... who prodded this country almost against its will to accept the challenge of change in the postwar years."

Henares studied in the best schools, Ateneo de Manila, University of the Philippines and the Massachusetts Institute of Technology, but his early schooling was in the public schools, where his Senator grandfather put him to prepare him for a political career; he became a cabinet member and a senatorial candidate together with Ninoy Aquino in 1967.

At the age of 30, he was already the head of a multi-million peso business enterprise. Henares became the President of the powerful Philippine Chamber of Industries, and eventually a member of the presidential cabinet as the Chairman of the National Economic Council and Presidential Assistant on Community Development. "One of the most brilliant of my cabinet," said President Diosdado Macapagal, the fifth President of the Philippine Republic.

Henares was at the age of 25, the dean of two graduate schools. He made one movie and it won the FAMAS Academy Award as the Best Documentary of the Year 1957. He sired six children, and was awarded the Presidential Award for Exemplary Family Life by Malacañang Palace in 1960. He was Young Businessman of the Year 1959 and Industrialist of the Year 1963.

He was a newspaper columnist (front page column "Ways and Means" in pre martial law Manila Times and in post-Edsa's "Make My Day!" in the Philippine Daily Inquirer, and in the Manila Standard), an essayist, a poet, a TV and radio commentator and a public speaker much in demand. He is now on UNTV owned by his son (UHF 37, Cable 58) at primetime 8:00 PM 5 days a week, Monday through Friday; and on radio DWBR-fm (104.3 Hz) six times daily (8:30 AM, 10:30 AM, 12:30 Noon, 2:30 PM, 4:30 PM, 6:30 PM) Monday through Friday. His website is www.philippinefolio.com.

He was the Presidential Consultant on National Affairs, to President Gloria Macapagal Arroyo whose father he served, and to President Fidel V. Ramos, a friend of his youth, who assigned him confidential tasks of national import, and took him along on State Visits. He was an Eisenhower Fellow in the USA, an official guest and negotiator of treaties in Great Britain, Israel, Germany, the People's Republic of China, Indonesia, Soviet Union, and an official representative to conferences abroad.

He is a radio amateur, a computer buff, an electronic expert who makes his own television sets, quadrophonic equipment, electronic organ, and burglar alarms; a photography and movie enthusiast; a gun and book collector.

Above all, he is a Nationalist in the great tradition of Claro M. Recto and Jose Rizal, an indefatigable champion of the nationalist cause, whose speeches and writings will show the way and the light for future generations of Filipinos. He is in 2016, an old man 92 years of age.

Books by Larry Henares, email job_elizes@yahoo.com
or access Amazon.com (books by Larry Henares)

Make My Day Series: of many essays on the Philippines
Kindle Edition, $ 3.00: Paperback, $12.00

Book 1: Make My Day	Book 2: Nice and Nasty
Book 3: Cecilia My Love	Book 4: Sweet and Sour
Book 5: Saints and Sinners	Book 6: Villains and Heroes
Book 7: Tough and Tender	Book 8: Light and Shadow
Book 9: Give and Take	Book 10: To Be or Not to Be
Book 11: Cash and Credits	Book 12: Rise and Fall
Book 13: Swans and Swine	Book 14: Touch and Go
Book 15: Life and Death	Book 16: Kiss and Bite
Book 17: Good and Evil	Book 18: Beast and Beauty
Book 19 Beggar and King	Book 20: Trash & Treasures
Book 21: Wear and Tear	Book 22 Angel and Devil
Book 23: Pretty Ugly	Book 24: Salvation & Damnation

Anthem Series: essays on the Philippines, old books

With Fervor Burning	Behold the Radiance
Suns and Stars Alight	For Us Thy Sons

Biographical Series: Kindle Edition $ 3.00, Paperback $12
Hilarion G. Henares: Life and Times, co-author Edith Perez de Tagle
Don Daniel Maramba: Life and Times, co-author Edith Perez de Tagle
The Moving Finger Writes: Love Letters

The Dawn of Great Civilizations:
Heralding the Return of the Mother Principle
51 pages of text and 51 pages of illustrations in full color, 8 ½ x 11
inches, Kindle Edition, $ 6.00; Paperback Edition, $ 30.00

The Sinatra Songbook, 1,300 lyrics, Kindle $ 3.00,
Paperback $ 15.00

Made in the USA
San Bernardino, CA
01 July 2017